Neighborho

Zona Gale

Alpha Editions

This edition published in 2022

ISBN: 9789356714069

Design and Setting By

Alpha Editions
www.alphaedis.com

Email - info@alphaedis.com

As per information held with us this book is in Public Domain.
This book is a reproduction of an important historical work.
Alpha Editions uses the best technology to reproduce historical work
in the same manner it was first published to preserve its original nature.
Any marks or number seen are left intentionally to preserve.

Contents

PREFACE	- 2 -
A GREAT TREE	- 8 -
EXIT CHARITY	- 21 -
THE TIME HAS COME	- 36 -
THE FACE OF FRIENDSHIP VILLAGE	- 53 -
THE FLOOD	- 70 -
THE PARTY	- 87 -
THE BIGGEST BUSINESS	- 100 -
THE PRODIGAL GUEST	- 116 -
MR. DOMBLEDON	- 121 -
HUMAN	- 138 -
THE HOME-COMING	- 147 -

To
**THE LITTLE TOWNS
OF
THE TIME TO COME**

PREFACE

"WHEN I die," said Calliope Marsh, "don't you get anybody that's always treated me like a dog and put them on the front seat. Make 'em sit back."

Then she looked at me, her rare and somewhat abashed smile on her face.

"Birds and stars and children and God in the world," she said, "and hark at me talking like that. Honest, I don't care where you seat 'em."

That is like Calliope. And that is like the village. Blunt and sometimes bitter speech there is, and now and again what we gently call "words"; but the faith of my experience is that these are facile, and need never trouble one. These are born of circumscription, of little areas, of teasing tasks, of lack of exercise, of that curious mingling which we call social life; but any one who takes seriously our faint feuds or even our narrow judgments does not know and love the Middle Western villages, nor understand that seeds and buds are not the norm of bloom. Instance, if you will, this case and that to show the contrary. But the days of pioneering, when folk drew together in defense, left us a heritage which no isolated instances can nullify. On the whole, we are all friends.

There could be no better basis for the changes that are upon us. The new ideals of the great world are here, in our little world. Though there is an impression to the contrary, the Zeitgeist is not attracted exclusively to cities. From design in our County Fair fancy work to our attitude toward the home, new things are come upon us. To be sure, we do not trust our power. We cling to our "Well, you can't change human nature" as to a recipe, though it does change before our eyes. If it were only that impossible plaques and pillows have given place to hammered brass and copper, our disregard might be warrantable. But now when one praises home life, home cooking, home training, home influence, we are beginning to say: "Whose home?" And the sentimentalities do not give place to reason without healthful cause. And when of late, from the barber's children's lunch basket, the young professor of our village took out the heavy, sunken biscuits of the barber's new wife and threw them in the ash box, even the barber's wrathful imprecations could not draw our sympathy to the side of the hearth, where once it would have stood upholding domestic unsanctities.

To be sure, in the village the old confusion between motherhood and domestic service still maintains. But both in cities and in villages perhaps it is to-morrow rather than to-day that we shall see women free from kitchen drudgery, and home economics a paid profession, such as nursing has lately become. Though when one of us said this, at a meeting of the Friendship Village Married Ladies' Cemetery Improvement Sodality, one of us rejoined:

"What! Do you mean that a womanly woman wants any occupation besides housekeeping? Why, I love my dishpan!"

And the burst of merriment which followed was almost a surprise to those who laughed, and to whom this extreme statement had unwittingly revealed the whole absurdity.

Already in the village it is almost impossible to get maids, even though many have entirely ceased to say "hired girl." Night after night we scan the Friendship Village Daily Paper (who shall read that name and not admit that we live close to the essentials?) and see the same half dozen "Wanted ... for General Housework" appeals drearily repeated. And while some of us merely wonder how "Mis' Whatever is getting along, and the weather what it is, and her baby not through the second summer," there are those of us who feel secret thanksgiving in the fact that we, too, are painfully playing our part in forcing the recognition of domestic service as an eight-hour-a-day profession. And "But who would answer the bell evenings?" and "Why, none of us could afford to keep help then!" sound as unreasoning as they did when apprentices first changed to clerks.

Even the village theology broadens before our eyes. Few can be found who do not admit the anomaly of denominationalism, even while they cling to it. And it is no longer considered reprehensible to state openly, as well as to believe secretly, that the truth about living which Jesus taught has been told in certain forms whose ancient interpretation no thinking person holds. Something of the glory of the God-ward striving of all religions is felt, here and there, in the village, and now and then, in a village sitting-room, you come on some one who is cherishing a vision like that of John on Patmos, and saying nothing.

To be sure, one village theologian was heard to cry:

"Empty or full, I tell you them churches are all necessary, every one of 'em. And if we had more kinds of 'em, then they'd be necessary too."

But there seemed to be something the matter with this. And on the whole there is more food for thought in another observation from among us:

"We always used to think Drug-store Curtsie was an infidel. And, land, there he is making the best State Senator we ever had. I guess we exaggerated it some, maybe."

We are beginning to be ashamed of charity and to see that our half dozen dependent families need not have been dependent, if their own gifts had been developed and their industry had not been ill-directed or exploited. And if that is true of the Rickers and the Hennings and the Hasketts and the Bettses and the Doles, we begin to suspect that it may be true of all poverty. We are beginning to be ashamed of many another inefficiency and folly which anciently we took for granted as necessary evils. Of his own product the village brewer says openly: "The time is coming when they won't let us make it. And I don't care how soon it comes." And this in the village, where we used to laugh at Keddie Bingy, drunken and singing on Daphne Street, and whose wife we censured for leaving him to shift for himself!

We are coming to applaud divorce when shame or faithlessness or disease or needless invalidism have attended marriage, and for a village woman to continue to earn her livelihood by marriage under these circumstances is now to her a disgrace hardly less evident than that of her city sister. We continue to cover up far too much, just as in the cities they cover too much. But we do mention openly things which in the old days we whispered or guessed at or whose peril we never knew at all. And when, by a visiting lecturer, more is admitted than we would ourselves admit, we are splendidly, if softly, triumphant with: "That couldn't have been done here twenty years ago."

To be sure, with some of the new terminology, we have had desperate battle.

"I don't like them eugenics," one of us said, "I know two of 'em that's separated."

Yet on the whole we tell one another that our new state law is "going to be" a good thing.

Inevitably, then, romance among us is becoming something else. The village girl no longer waits at the gate in a blue sash. There are no gates. She is wearing belts. And I heard one of the girls of the village say:

"A girl used to act so silly about being happy. What did she mean by that—being made love to forever by somebody forever in love with her? Well, I want something more than that in mine."

And there, in her vague, slang speech lay the outline of the shadow that is pointing women to share in the joys of the race and the delight of a chosen occupation. And though not many of us here in the village will say as much as that, yet genetically the thing goes on: Women choose occupations, develop gifts, sail for Europe, refuse "good offers" even if these do hold out "support," or come out with fine, open hatred of the menial tasks which their "womanliness" once forbade them to disavow. And beyond, in all relevancy, there opens the knowledge that motherhood is a thing to be trained for, as much as stenography!

Yet meadows sweet with hay, and twilights, and firelight, and the home (around the evening lamp) have not passed; but they lie close to a Romance of Life now coming fast upon us, away here in the village—a Romance of Life as much finer than sentimentality as modern romance is saner than chivalry.

In spite of our Armory and our strong young guard, we are quite simply for peace, and believe that it will come. And because we have among us a few of other races whom we understand, race prejudice is a thing which never troubles us; and I think that we could slip into the broadened race concept without realizing that anything had happened. The only thunder of change which does not echo here is the thunder of the industrial conflict. But although most of the village takes sides quite naïvely with the newspaper headlines, yet that is chiefly because the thing lies beyond our experience, and because—like the dwellers in cities—we lack imagination to visualize what is occurring. As far as our experience goes, the most of us are democratic. But when there arises an issue transcending our experience, our tendency is to uncompromising conservatism. And there is hope in the fact that politically many of us are free and think for ourselves, and smile at the abuse that is heaped upon great leaders, and understand with thanksgiving—away here in the village—how often the demagogues of to-day are the demi-gods of to-morrow.

We well know that with all this changing attitude, we are losing a certain homely flavor. Old possibilities, especially of humor, no longer have incidence. Our sophistication somehow includes our laughter. In these days, in what village could it happen, at the funeral of a well-beloved townsman, with the church filled to do him honor, that the minister should open his eyes at the close of the prayer, and absently say:

"The contribution will now be received."

Yet that and the consequent agonized signaling of one of the elders are within my memory, and are indelibly there because they occurred at the first funeral in my experience, and I could not account for the elder's perturbation.

Or, where among us now is the village dignitary who would take the platform to speak at the obsequies of a friend and would begin his eulogy with:

"I have always had a great respect for the deceased, for—[pointing with his thumb downward at the coffin] for that gentleman down there."

Or, when a deacon with squeaking shoes is passing the plate, in what modern village church is to be found the clergyman who will call out:

"Brother, you'll find my rubbers there in the lecture room. You best slip 'em on."

Or the deacon who would instantly reply, overshoulder:

"I've got a pair of me own," and so go serenely on, squeaking, to the last pew.

Yet these happened, not long ago, and we smile at the remembrance, knowing that just those things could not take place among us now. New absurdities occur. But there is a different humor, even of misadventure and the maladroit. Instead of deploring the old days, however, I think that nearly all of us say what I have heard a woman of ninety saying—not, "Things are not what they used to be in the old days," but:

"Well, I'm thankful that I've lived to see so many things different."

That is the way in which we grow old in the little towns of the Middle West. We are not afraid to know that old ways of laughter and old flavors of incident depart, with the old ills. Since disease and marching armies and the like are to leave us, humor and sentimentalism of a sort and gold lace of many sorts must likewise be foregone. We say: "The day is dead. Long be the day." May we not boast of it? For such adaptation would not be wonderful in a city, where impressions crowd and are cut off. But it stands for a special and precious form of vitality, in little towns.

It is for this acceptance of growth that our days of pioneering together and our slow drawing together of later years form a solid basis. For we are knit, and now the fabric is beginning to be woven into a garment. Some are alarmed at the lack of seams, some *anxiously question the color, some shake their heads and say that it will never fit. But there are those of us here in the village who think that we understand.*

And now we are beginning to suspect that there is more to understand than we have guessed. For there was some one "From Away" who came to us and said:

"Your little town is a piece of to-morrow. Once a village was a source of quiet and content and prettiness. Once a village was withdrawn from what is going forward in the world. But now the village is the very source of our salvation, social and artistic. It is not that we are finding humanity at its best in the villages, but that there humanity is at the point where it is most in type. And in this lie the hidings of our power."

We listened, not all of us believing. We were used to being praised for our cedar fenceposts, our mossy roofs, our bothersome, low-hanging elm boughs, even, of late, for our irregular streets and our creamy brick. But in our hearts we had been feeling apologetic that we had not more two-storey shops, not more folk who go away in Summer, and not even one limousine. And now we were hearing that we are playing a part social, artistic, which no city can play!

It is true that from the days of those old happenings which I have been recounting, down to now, the form of our self-expression has changed somewhat, its quality, never. Always we have been ourselves, simply and unreservedly. Not boldly ourselves, for we do not know that there is anything to be bold about. But in the small things, quite simply ourselves. And once I would have called that a negative quality....

But what of this salvation, social and artistic, and how are these to be fostered by our one characteristic? And with that, the cries of the world, from art, from life, are in one's ears: Against imitation, against artificiality, against seeing the thing as a thousand others have seen it and saying it as a thousand others have said it, against moving in a mass which has won the right to no social adhesion, but instead stupidly coheres, and does its thinking by bad proxies. And we—who do already let ourselves be ourselves—who knows what contribution we may be bringing, now that there have come upon us these new reactions to convention, these slow new freedoms of belief?

There in the cities, humanity is in the melting pot, we say; and the figure is that of countless specializations dissolved in one general mass. We revert to type individually, but we advance to type collectively. Unquestionably this collective advance is a part of experience. But it is not an ultimate of experience. Somewhere there beyond, shining, is a new individualism, whose incarnations shall flow to no melting pot, but instead shall cling together, valued for their differentiation, and like a certain precious form of life, low in the scale, shall put out a thousand filaments, and presently move away together, a unit.

Already the individual experiences this progression—that is, he does if he does!— and, through his own unique value, wins back in later life to that simplicity which is every one's birthright. It is Nietzsche's threefold metamorphosis of the spirit: First the camel, then the lion, last the child. What if, standing in that simplicity, at the point where humanity is most in type, the village does open the social and artistic outlook of Tomorrow?

Some of us believe. Some of us say: "What if the federation of the world is to begin in the little towns? What if it is beginning there now...."

"A village is nothing but a little something broke off from a city," says Calliope Marsh, "only it never started in hitched to the city in the first place. And that makes all the difference."

It is Calliope Marsh who tells, in her own speech, these Neighborhood Stories. And if she were given to selecting texts, I think that she would have selected one which says that life is something other than that which we believe it to be.

PORTAGE,   WISCONSIN,
    August, 1914.

A GREAT TREE

I NEVER had felt so much like Christmas, said Calliope Marsh, as I did that year.

"I wish't," I says, when it got 'most time, "I wish't I knew somebody to have a Christmas tree with."

"Well, Calliope Marsh," says Mis' Postmaster Sykes, looking surprised-on-purpose, the way she does, "ain't there enough poor and neglected folks in this world to please anybody?"

"I didn't say have a Christmas tree *for*," I says back at her; "I says have one *with*."

"I don't know what you mean by that difference," she says, "I'm sure."

"I donno," I says, "as I know either. But there is a difference, somewhere. I'd kind of like to have a tree *with* folks this year."

"Why don't you help on your church tree?" Mis' Sykes ask' me. "They're going to spend quite a little money on theirs this year."

"I hate to box Christmas up in a church," I says.

"Why, Calliope Marsh!" she says, shocked.

I didn't want to hurt her feelings—I ain't never one of those that likes to throw their ideas in folks's faces and watch folks jump back. So I tried to talk about something else, but she went right on, trying her best to help me out.

"The ward schools is each going to have a tree this year, I hear," she says. "Why don't you go in on your ward, Calliope, and help out there? They'd be real glad of help, you know."

"I hate to divide Christmas off into wards," I says to her.

"Well, then, go in with a family," she says; "any of us'll be real glad to have you," she adds, generous. "*We* would. Come to ours—we're going to have a great big tree for the children. I've been stringing the pop-corn and cutting the paper for it whenever I got an odd minute. The Holcombs, they're going to have one too—and Mis' Uppers and Mis' Merriman and even the Hubbelthwaits and Abigail Arnold, for her little nieces. I never see a year when everybody was going to celebrate so nice. Come on with one of us, why don't you?"

"Well," I says, "mebbe I will. I'll see. I don't know yet what I will do," I told her. And I went off down the street. What I wanted to say was, "I hate to box Christmas up in a family," but I didn't quite dare—yet.

Friendship Village ain't ever looked much more like Christmas, to my notion, than it did that December. Just the right snow had come—and no more; and just the right cold—and no more. The moon was getting along so's about the night of the twenty-fifth it was going to loom up big and gold and warm over the fields on the flats, where it always comes up in winter like it had just edged around there to get sort of a wide front yard for its big show, where the whole village could have a porch seat.

You know when you live in a village you always know whether the moon is new or to the full or where it is and when it's going to be; but when you live in a city you just look up in the sky some night and say "Oh, that's so, there's the moon," and go right on thinking about something else. Here in the village that December everything was getting ready, deliberate, for a full-moon Christmas, like long ago. The moon and the cold and the snow, and all them public things, was doing their best, together, for our common Christmas. All but us. It seemed like all of us humans was working for it separate.

Tramping along there in the snow that night, I thought over what Mis' Sykes had said, and about all the places she'd mentioned over was going to have Christmas trees. And I looked along to the houses, most of 'em lying right there on Daphne Street, where they were going to have 'em—I could see 'em all, one tree after another, lighted and streaming from house to house all up and down Daphne Street, just the way they were going to look.

And then there was the little back streets, and the houses down on the flats, where there wouldn't be any trees nor much of any Christmas. Of course, as Mis' Sykes had said, the poor and the neglected are always with us—yet; but I didn't want to pounce down on any of 'em with a bag of fruit and a box of animal crackers and set and watch 'em.

That wasn't what I meant by having a Christmas *with* somebody.

"There'd ought to be some place—" I was beginning to think, when right along where I was, by the Market Square, I come on five or six children, kicking around in the snow. It was 'most dark, but I could just make 'em out: Eddie Newhaven, Arthur Mills, Lily Dorron, and two-three more.

"Hello, folks," I says, "what you doing? Having a carnival?" Because it's on the Market Square that carnivals and some little circuses and things that belongs to everybody is usually celebrated.

Little Arthur Mills spoke up. "No," he says, "we was just playing we's selling a load of Christmas trees."

"Christmas trees," I says. "Why, that's so. This is where they always bring 'em to sell—big load of 'em for everybody, ain't it?"

"They're going to bring an *awful* big load here this time," says Eddie Newhaven—"big enough for everybody in town to have one. Most of the fellows is going to have 'em—us and Ned Backus and the Cartwrights and Joe Tyrril and Lifty—all of 'em."

"My," I says, "what a lot of Christmas trees! Why, if they was set along by the curbstone here on Daphne Street," I says, just to please the children and make a little talk with 'em, "why, the line of 'em would reach all up and down the town," I says. "Wouldn't that be fun?"

Little Lily claps her hands.

"Oh, yes," she cries, "wouldn't that be fun? With pop-corn strings all going from one to the other?"

"It would be a grand sight," says I, looking down across the Market Square. There, hanging all gold and quiet, like it didn't think it amounted to much, right over the big cedar-of-Lebanon-looking tree in the Square, was the moon, crooked to a horn.

"Once," says Eddie Newhaven, "when they was selling the Christmas trees here, they kept right on selling 'em after dark. And they stood 'em around here and put a little light in each one. It was awful nice. Wouldn't it be nice if they'd do that all over the Square some time!"

"It would be a grand sight," says I again, "but one that the folks in this town would never have time for...."

While I spoke I was looking down across Market Square again toward the moon hanging over the cedar-of-Lebanon-looking tree.

"There's a pretty good-looking tree there already," I says idle. "What a grand thing it would be lit up," says I, for not much of any reason—only to keep the talk going with the children. Then something went through me from my head to my feet. "Why not light it some time?" I says.

The children set up a little shout—part because they liked it, part because they thought such a thing could never be. I laughed with 'em, and I went on up the street—but all the time something in me kept on saying something, all hurried and as if it meant it. And little ends of ideas, and little jagged edges of other ideas, and plans part raveled out that you thought you could knit up again, and long, sharp motions, a little something like light, kept going through my head and going through it.

Down to the next corner I met Ben Cory, that keeps the livery-stable and sings bass to nearly everybody's funeral and to other public occasions.

"Ben," I says excited, though I hadn't thought anything about this till that minute, "Ben—you getting up any Christmas Eve Christmas carols to sing this year?"

He had a new string of sleigh-bells over his shoulder, and he give it a shift, I recollect, so's they all jingled.

"Well," he says, "I did allow to do it. But I've spoke to one or two, and they donno's they can do it. Some has got to sing to churches earlier in the evening and they donno's they want to tune up all night. And the most has got to be home for family Christmas."

"There ain't," I says, "no manner o' doubt about the folks that'd be glad to listen, is there, provided you had the singers?"

"Oh, sure," he says. "Folks shines up to music consider'ble, Christmas Eve. It—sort of—well, it——"

"Yes," I says, "I know. It does, don't it? Well, Ben Cory, you get your Christmas-carol singers together and a-caroling, and I'll undertake that there sha'n't nothing much stand in the way of their being out on Christmas Eve. Is it a bargain?"

His face lit up, all jolly and hearty.

"Why, sure it's a bargain," he says. "I'll get 'em. I wanted to, only I didn't want to carol 'em any more than they wanted to be caroled. I'll get 'em," he says, and gives his bells a hunch that made 'em ring all up and down Daphne Street—that the moon was looking down at just as if it was public property and not all made up of little private plans with just room enough for us four and no more, or figures to that effect.

I donno if you've ever managed any kind of a revolution?

They's two kinds of revolutions. One breaks off of something that's always been. You pick up the broke piece and try to throw it away to make room for something that's growing out of the other part. And 'most everybody will begin to tell you that the growing piece ain't any good, but that the other part is the kind you have always bought and that you'd better save it and stick it back on. But then they's the other kind of revolution that backs away from something that's always been and looks at it a little farther off than it ever see it before, and says: "Let's us move a little way around and pay attention to this thing from a new spot." And real often, if you put it that way, they's enough people willing to do that, because they know they can go right back afterward and stand in the same old place if they want to.

Well, this last was the kind of a revolution I took charge of that week before Christmas. I got my plans and my ideas and my notions all planned and thought and budded, and then I presented 'em around, abundant.

The very next morning after I'd seen the children I started out, while I had kind of a glow to drape around the difficulties so's I couldn't see 'em. I went first to the store-keepers, seeing Christmas always seems to hinge and hang on what they say and do. And I went to Eppleby Holcomb, because I knew he'd see it like I done—and I wanted the brace of being agreed with, like you do.

Eppleby's store was all decorated up with green cut paper and tassels and turkey-red calico poinsettias, and it looked real nice and tasty. And the store was full of the country trade. The little overhead track that took the bundles had broke down just at the wrong minute, and old rich Mis' Wiswell's felt soles had got stuck half-way, and Eppleby himself was up on top of a counter trying to rescue 'em for her, while she made tart remarks below. When he'd fished 'em out and wrapped 'em up for her,

"Eppleby," I says, "would you be willing to shut up shop on Christmas Eve, or wouldn't you?"

He looked kind of startled. "It's a pretty good night for trade, you know, Calliope?" says he—doubtful.

"Why, yes," I says, "it is. But everybody that's going to give presents to people'll give presents to people. And if the stores ain't open Christmas Eve, folks'll buy 'em when the stores *is* open. Is that sense, or ain't it?"

He knew it was. And when I told him what I'd got hold of, stray places in my head, he says if the rest would shut he'd shut, and be glad of it. Abigail Arnold done the same about her home bakery, and the Gekerjecks, and two-three more. But Silas Sykes, that keeps the post-office store, he was firm.

"If that ain't woman-foolish," he says, "I donno what is. You ain't no more idee of business than so many cats. No, sir. I don't betray the public by cutting 'em off of one evening's shopping like that."

It made a nice little sentence to quote, and I quoted it consider'ble. And the result was, the rest of 'em, that knew Silas, head and heart, finally says, all right, he could keep open if he wanted to, and enjoy himself, and they'd all shut up. I honestly think they kind of appreciated, in a nice, neighborly way, making Silas feel mean—when he'd ought to.

It was a little harder to make the Sunday-school superintendents see the thing that I had in my head. Of course, when a thing has been the way it has been for a good while, you can't really blame people for feeling that it's been the way it ought to be. Feelings seems made that way. Our superintendent has been our superintendent for 'most forty years—ever since the church was built—and of course his thoughts is kind of turned to bone in some places, naturally.

His name is Jerry Bemus, and he keeps a little harness shop next door to the Town Hall that's across from Market Square. When I went in that day he was resting from making harnesses, and he was practising on his cornet. He can make a bugle call real nice—you can often hear it, going up and down Daphne Street in the morning, and when I'm down doing my trading I always like to hear it—it gives me kind of a nice, old-fashioned feeling, like when Abigail Arnold fries doughnuts in the back of the Home Bakery and we can all smell 'em, out in the road.

"Jerry," I says, "how much is our Sunday-school Christmas tree going to cost us?"

Jerry's got a wooden leg, and he can *not* remember not to try to cross it over the other one. He done that now, and give it up.

"We calc'late about twenty-five dollars," says he, proud.

"What we going to do to celebrate?"

"Well," he says, "have speaking pieces—we got a program of twenty numbers already," says he, pleased. "And a trimmed tree, and an orange, and a bag of nuts and candy for every child," he says.

"All the other churches is going to do the same," I says. "Five trees and five programs and five sets of stuff all around. And all of 'em on Christmas Eve, when you'd think we'd all sort of draw together instead of setting apart, in cliques. Land," I says out, "that first Christmas Eve wouldn't the angels have stopped singing and wept in the sky if they could of seen what we'd do to it!"

"Hush, Calliope," says Jerry Bemus, shocked. "They ain't no need to be sacrilegious, is they?"

"Not a bit," says I; "we've been it so long a'ready, worshiping around in sections like Hottentots. Well, now," I says, "do you honestly think we've all chose the best way to go at Christmas Eve for the children, filling them up with colored stuff and getting their stummicks all upset?"

We had quite a little talk about it, back and forth, Jerry and me. And all of a sudden, while I was trying my best to make him see what I saw, I happened to notice his bugle again.

"There ain't no thrill in none of it," I was saying to him. "Not half so much," I says, "as there is in your bugle. When I hear that go floating up and down the street, I always kind of feel like it was announcing something. To my notion," I says, "it could announce Christmas to this town far better than forty-'leven little separate trimmed-up trees.... Why, Jerry," I says out sudden, "listen to what I've thought of...."

A little something had come in my head that minute, unexpected, that fitted itself into the rest of my plan. And it made Jerry say, pretty soon, that he was willing to go with me to see the other superintendents; and we done so that very day. Ain't it funny how big things work out by homely means—by homely means? Sole because the choir-leader in one choir had resigned because the bass in that choir was the bass in that choir, and so they didn't have anybody there to train their Christmas music, and sole because another congregation was hard up and was having to borrow its Christmas celebration money out of the foreign missionary fund—we got 'em to see sense. And then the other two joined in.

The schools were all right from the first, being built, like they are, on a basis of belonging to everybody, same as breathing and one-two other public utilities, and nothing dividing anybody from anybody. And I begun to feel like life and the world was just one great bud, longing to open, so be it could get enough care.

The worst ones to get weaned away from a perfectly selfish way of observing Christ's birthday was the private families. Land, land, I kept saying to myself them days, we all of us act like we was studying kindergarten mathematics. We count up them that's closest to us, and we can't none of us seem to count much above ten.

Not all of 'em was that way, though. Well—if it just happens that you live in any town whatever in the civilized world, I think you'll know about what I had said to me.

On the one hand it went about like this, from Mis' Timothy Toplady and the Holcombs and the Hubbelthwaits and a lot more:

"Well, land knows, it'd save us lots of back-aching work—but—will the children like it?"

"Like it?" I says. "Try 'em. Trust 'em without trying 'em if you want to. I would. Remember," I couldn't help adding, "you like to be with the children a whole lot oftener than they like to be with you. What they like is to be together."

And, "Well, do you honestly think it'll work? I don't see how it can—anything so differ'nt."

And, "Well, they ain't any harm trying it one year, as I can see. That can't break up the holidays, as I know of."

But the other side had figured it out just like the other side of everything always figures.

"Calliope," says Mis' Postmaster Sykes, "are you crazy-headed? What's your idee? Ain't things all right the way they've always been done?"

"Well," says I, conservative, "not all of 'em. Not wholesale, I wouldn't say."

"But you can't go changing things like this," she told me. "What'll become of Christmas?"

"Christmas," I says, "don't need you or me, Mis' Sykes, to be its guardians. All Christmas needs is for us to get out of its way, and leave it express what it means."

"But the *home* Christmas," she says, 'most like a wail. "Would you do away with that?"

Then I sort of turned on her. I couldn't help it.

"Whose home?" I says stern. "If it's your home you mean, or any of the thousands of others like it where Christmas is kept, then you know, and they all know, that nothing on earth can take away the Christmas feeling and the Christmas joy as long as you want it to be there. But if it's the homes you mean—and there's thousands of 'em—where no Christmas ever comes, you surely ain't arguing to keep them the way they've been kept?"

But she continued to shake her head.

"You can do as you like, of course," she said, "and so can everybody else. It's their privilege. But as for me, I shall trim my little tree here by our own fireside. And here we shall celebrate Christmas—Jeddie and Nora and father and me."

"Why can't you do *both*?" I says. "I wouldn't have you give up your fireside end of things for anything on earth. But why can't you do both?"

Mis' Sykes didn't rightly seem to know—at least she didn't say. But she give me to understand that her mind run right along in the self-same groove it had had made for it, cozy.

Somehow, the longer I live, the less sense I seem to have. There's some things I've learned from twenty-five to thirty times in my life, and yet I can't seem to remember them no more than I can remember whether it's sulphite or sulphate of soda that I take for my quinsy. And one of these is about taking things casual.

That night, for instance, when I come round the corner on to Daphne Street at half-past seven on Christmas Eve, I thought I was going to have to waste a minute or two standing just where the bill-board makes a shadow for the arc-light, trying to get used to the idea of what we were doing—used to it in my throat. But there wasn't much time to spend that way, being there were things to do between then and eight o'clock, when we'd told 'em all to be there. So I ran along and tried not to think about it—except the work part. 'Most always, the work part of anything'll steady you.

The great cedar-of-Lebanon-looking tree, standing down there on the edge of the Market Square and acting as if it had been left from some long-ago forest, on purpose, had been hung round with lines and lines of strung pop-corn—the kind that no Christmas tree would be a Christmas tree without, because so many, many folks has set up stringing it nights of Christmas week, after the children was in bed, and has kept it, careful, in a box, so's it'd do for next year. We had all that from the churches—Methodist and Presbyterian and Episcopal and Baptist and Catholic pop-corn, and you couldn't tell 'em apart at all when you got 'em on the tree. The festoons showed ghostly-white in the dark and the folks showed ghostly-black, hurrying back and forth doing the last things.

And the folks was coming—you could hear 'em all along Daphne Street, tripping on the bad place that hadn't been mended because it was right under the arc-light, and coming over the hollow-sounding place by Graham's drug-store, and coming from the little side streets and the dark back streets and the streets down on the flats. Some of 'em had Christmas trees waiting at home—the load had been there on the Market Square, just like we had let it be there for years without seeing that the Market Square had any other Christmas uses—and a good many had bought trees. But a good many more had decided not to have any—only just to hang up stockings; and to let the great big common Christmas tree stand for what it stood for, gathering most of that little garland of Daphne Street trees up into its living heart.

Over by the bandstand I come on them I'd been looking for—Eddie Newhaven and Arthur Mills and Lily Dorron and Sarah and Mollie and the Cartwrights and Lifty and six-eight more.

"Hello, folks," I says. "What you down here for? Why ain't you home?"

They answered all together:

"For the big tree!"

"Are you, now?" I says—just to keep on a-talking to 'em. "Whose tree?"

I love to remember the way they answered. It was Eddie Newhaven that said it.

"Why, all of us's!" he said.

All of us's! I like to say it over when they get to saying "mine" and "theirs" too hard where I am.

When it was eight o'clock and there was enough gathered on the Square, they done the thing that was going to be done, only nobody had known how well they were going to do it. They touched the button, and from the bottom branch to the tip-top little cone, the big old tree came alight, just like it knew what it was all about and like it had come out of the ground long ago for this reason—only we'd never known. Two hundred little electric lights there were, colored, and paid for private, though I done my best to get the town to pay for 'em, like it ought to for its own tree; but they was paid for private—yet.

It made a little *oh!* come in the crowd and run round, it was so big and beautiful, standing there against the stars like it knew well enough that it was one of 'em, whether we knew it or not. And coming up across the flats, big and gold and low, was the moon, most full, like *it* belonged, too.

"And glory shone around," I says to myself—and I stood there feeling the glory, outside and in. Not my little celebration, and your little celebration, and their little celebration, private, that was costing each of us more than it ought to—but our celebration, paying attention to the message that Christ paid attention to.

I was so full of it that I didn't half see Ben Cory and his carolers come racing out of the dark. They was all fixed up in funny pointed hoods and in cloaks and carrying long staves with everybody's barn-yard lanterns tied on the end of 'em, and they run out in a line down to the tree, and they took hold of hands and danced around it, singing to their voices' top a funny old tune, one of them tunes that, whether you've ever heard it before or not, kind of makes things in you that's older than you are yourself wake up and remember, real plain.

And Jerry Bemus shouted out at 'em: "Sing it again—sing it again!" and pounded his wooden leg with his cane. "Sing it again, I tell you. I ain't heard anybody sing that for goin' on forty years." And everybody laughed, and they sung it again for him, and some more songs that had come out of the old country that a little bit of it was living inside everybody that was there. And while they were singing, it came to me all of a sudden about another night, 'most three hundred years before, when on American soil that lonesome English heart, up there in Boston, had dreamed ahead to a time when Christmas would come here....

"But faith unrolls the future scrolls;
Christmas shall not die,
Nor men of English blood and speech
Forget their ancestry—"

or any other blood, or any other speech that has in it the spirit of what Christ come to teach. And that's all of us. And it felt to me as if now we were only just beginning to take out our little single, lonely tapers and carry them to light a great tree.

Then, just after the carols died down, the thing happened that we'd planned to happen: Over on one side the choirs of all the churches, that I guess had never sung together in their lives before, though they'd been singing steadily about the self-same things since they was born choirs, begun to sing—

Silent night, holy night.

Think of it—down there on the Market Square that had never had anything sung on it before except carnival tunes and circus tunes. All up and down Daphne Street it must of sounded, only there was hardly anybody far off to hear it, the most of 'em being right there with all of us. They sung it without anybody playing it for 'em and they sung it from first to last.

And then they slipped into another song that isn't a Christmas carol exactly, nor not any song that comes in the book under "Christmas," but something that comes in just as natural as if it was another name for what Christmas was—"Nearer, my God, to thee," and "Lead, Kindly Light," and some more. And after a bar or two of the first one, the voices all around begun kind of mumbling and humming and carrying the tunes along in their throats without anybody in particular starting 'em there, and then they all just naturally burst out and sung too.

And so I donno who done it—whether the choirs had planned it that way, or whether they just thought of it then, or whether somebody in the crowd struck it up unbeknownst to himself, or whether the song begun to sing itself; but it come from somewhere, strong and clear and real—a song that the children has been learning in school and has been teaching the town for a year or two now, sung to the tune of "Wacht am Rhein":

The crest and crowning of all good—
Life's common goal—is brotherhood.

And then everybody sung. Because that's a piece you can't sing alone. You can *not* sing it alone. All over the Market Square they took it up, and folks that couldn't sing, and me that can't sing a note except when there's nobody around that would recognize me if they ever saw me again—we all sung together, there in the dark, with the tree in the midst.

And we seemed long and long away from the time when the leader in one of them singing choirs had left the other choir because the bass in the other choir was the bass in the other choir. And it was like the Way Things Are had suddenly spoke for a minute, there in the singing choirs come out of their separate lofts, and in all the singing folks. And in all of us—all of us.

Then up hopped Eppleby Holcomb on to a box in front of the tree, and he calls out:

"Merry Christmas! Merry Christmas—on the first annual outdoor Christmas-tree celebration of Friendship Village!"

When he said that I felt—well, it don't make any difference to anybody how I felt; but what I done was to turn and make for the edge of the crowd just as fast as I could. And just then there come what Eppleby's words was the signal for. And out on the little flagstaff balcony of the Town Hall Jerry Bemus stepped with his bugle, and he blew it shrill and clear, so that it sounded all over the town, once, twice, three times, a bugle-call to say it was Christmas. We couldn't wait till twelve o'clock—we are all in bed long before that time in Friendship Village, holiday or not.

But the bugle-call said it was Christmas just the same. Think of it ... the bugle that used to say it was war. And the same minute the big tree went out, all still and quiet, but to be lit again next year and to stay a living thing in between.

When I stepped on to Daphne Street, who should I come face to face with but Mis' Postmaster Sykes. I was feeling so glorified over, that I never thought of its being strange that she was there. But she spoke up, just the same as if I'd said: "Why, I thought you wasn't coming near."

"The children was bound to come," she says, "so I had to bring 'em."

"Yes," I thought to myself, "the children know. They know."

And I even couldn't feel bad when I passed the post-office store and see Silas sitting in there all sole alone—the only lit store in the street. I knew he'd be on the Market Square the next year.

They went singing through all the streets that night, Ben Cory and his carolers. "Silent night, holy night" come from my front gate when I was 'most asleep. It was like the whole town was being sung to by something that didn't show. And when the time comes that this something speaks clear all the time,—well, it ain't a very far-off time, you know.

EXIT CHARITY

"Yes, sir," said Silas Sykes, "we got to get some charity goin' in this town."

"Charity," I says over, meditative. "How do you mean, Silas?"

"How do I mean?" says Silas, snappy. "Don't you know your Bible, woman?"

"I ain't so sure I do as I use' to be," I told him. "I use' to think charity was givin' things away. Then I had a spell I use' to think it was coverin' up their faults. Now I dunno as I'm clear what it is."

Silas bridled some and snorted soft.

"Charity," says he, "charity, Calliope Marsh, is doin' nice things for folks."

"Doin' nice things for folks," I says over—and I wanted to remember them words of Silas and I longed to feed 'em to him some time. But I just took up my pound of prunes and went out the post-office store, thoughtful.

Outside on the walk, I come on Absalom. He stood kicking his heels on the hydrant and looking up and down the street like he was waiting, for something that there wasn't any such thing, and he knew it. Absalom Ricker he was, that has work in the canning factory, when any. I'd been wantin' to see him.

"Evenin', Ab," says I. "How's Gertie?"

"She ain't on her feet yet," says he, rueful.

"How's your mother's rheumatism?"

"It ain't in her fingers yet," says he, bright.

"How're you?"

"Oh, me!" he says. "I'm rosy."

"Your arm," says I; "will it let you go to work yet?"

"Not yet," he says, "the thermometer actin' up zero, so. But still, I'm rosy—rosy."

"Well," says I, "bein' you're more rosy than busy, I wonder if you couldn't do something for us ladies. You know," I says, "that nice, new, galvanized iron garbage tank us ladies bought and run one season, collectin' up garbage? Well, I dunno but what we've got to sell it, the Council refusin' to run it, 'count of economy. And I wondered if you'd go and hev a look at it, and tell us what we'd ought to get for it, and where."

"Why, sure I will," says Absalom. "I'd be glad," says he, kind of pleasant and important, "to accommodate."

He went off down the street, walking sidewise, like he does, his coat and beard blowing out the same side, his pockets sagging till they looked like mouths smiling, and his hat trained up to a peak. Everybody liked Absalom—he had such a nice, one-sided smile and he seemed to be so afraid he was going to hurt your feelings. He'd broke his right arm in Silas's canning factory that fall, and he'd been laying off ever since. His wife done washings, and his mother finished vests from the city, and the children stuffed up cracks in the walls and thought it was a game.

They was others in the town, come lately, and mostly in the factory, that was the same way: the Bettses and the Doles and the Haskitts and the Hennings. They lived in little shacks around, and the men worked in the canning factory and the gas-works and on the tracks, and the women helped out. And one or two of 'em had took down ill; and so it was Silas, that likes to think of things first, that up and said "do something." And it was him put the notice in the papers a few nights later to all citizens—and women—that's interested in forming a Charity Society to meet in Post-Office Hall, that he has the renting of.

I was turning in the stairway to the hall that night when I heard somebody singing. And coming down the walk, with her hat on crooked and its feather broke, was old Bess Bones. Bess has lived in Friendship Village for years—and I always thought it was real good for the town that she done so. For she is the only woman I ever knew of that ain't respectable, and ain't rich or famous either, and yet that goes to everybody's house.

She does cleaning and scrubbing, and we all like to get her to do it, she does it so thoroughly conscientious. She brings us in little remedies she knows about, and vegetables from her own garden, and eggs. Sometimes some of us asks her to set down to a meal. Once she brought me a picked chicken of hers. And it's good for Friendship Village because we all see she's human, and mostly with women like that we build a thick wall and don't give 'em a chance to even knock out a brick ever after.

"I was just goin' to see you, Miss Marsh," she says. "I got kind o' lonesome and I thought I'd bring you over a begonia slip and set a while."

"I'm sorry, Bess," I says. "I'm going to a meeting."

"What kind of meetin'?" she says. "P'litical?"

"Yes," I says, "something like that." And that was true, of course, being politics is so often carried on by private charity from the candidates.

"I'd kind of like to go to a meeting again," she says, wistful. "I sung to revival meetings for a month once, when I was a girl."

"I guess you wouldn't like this one," I says. "Come to see me tomorrow and I'll tell you about it."

And then I went up-stairs and left her standing there on the sidewalk, and I felt kind of ashamed and sneaking. I didn't know why. But I says to myself, comforting, that she'd probably of broke out and sung in the middle of the meeting, if she had come. Her head ain't right, like the most of ours; but hers takes noisy forms, so you notice more.

Eleven of us turned out to the meeting, which was a pretty good proportion, there being only fifteen hundred living in Friendship Village all together. Silas was in the chair, formal as a funeral.

"The idear, as I understand it," says Silas, when the meeting was open, "is to get some Charity going. We'd ought to organize."

"And then what?" asks Mis' Toplady.

"Why, commence distributin' duds and victuals," says Silas.

"Well-a," says Mis' Toplady, "and keep on distributing them all our lives?"

"Sure," says Silas, "unless you're goin' to be weary in well-doing. Them folks'll keep right on being hungry and nekked as long as they live."

"Why will they?" says Mis' Toplady, puzzled.

"Well, they're poor folks, ain't they?" says Silas, scowling.

"Why, yes," says Mis' Toplady; "but that ain't all they is to 'em, is it?"

"What do you *mean*?" says Silas.

"Why, I mean," says Mis' Toplady, "can't they be got goin' so's they sha'n't *be* poor folks?"

Silas used his face like he smelled something. "Don't you know no more about folks than that?" says he. "Facts is facts. You've got to take folks as they are."

"But you ain't taking folks nowheres. You're leavin' 'em as they are, Silas," says Mis' Toplady, troubled.

Mis' Silas Sykes spoke up with her way of measuring off just enough for everybody.

"It's this way Silas means," she says. "Folks are rich, or medium, or poor. We've got to face that. It's always been so."

Mis' Toplady kind of bit at her lower lip a few times in a way she has, that wrinkles up her nose meditative. "It don't follow out," she says, firm. "My back yard used to be all chickweed. Now it's pure potatoes."

"Folks," says Mis' Sykes, real witherin', "folks ain't dirt."

"That's what I thought," says Mis' Toplady, dry.

Silas went right over their heads, like he does.

"We've all been doin' what we could for these folks," he says, "but we ain't been doin' it real wise. It's come to my notice that the Haskitts had four different chickens give to 'em last Christmas. What we want to do is to fix up some sort of a organization so's our chickens won't lap."

"Well," says Timothy Toplady, "then let's organize. That ain't hard. I move it be done."

It was done, and Silas was made president, like he ever loves to be, and Timothy treasurer, and me secretary, because they could get me to take it.

"Now," says Silas, "let's get down to work and talk over cases."

"*Cases?*" says Mis' Toplady, distasteful. "They ain't got the smallpox, have they? Say *folks*."

"I guess you ain't very used to Charity societies," says Silas, tolerant. "Take the Haskitts. They ain't got a pane o' glass in their house."

"Nor no wood, much," says Timothy. "When I went to get the rent the cat was asleep on the cook-stove."

"What rent do they give you, Timothy?" says Silas.

"Five dollars," he says, pursin' his lips.

"That's only three per cent. on the money. I don't see how you can afford it."

"I *am* indulgin' myself a little," Timothy admits. "But I been thinkin' o' raisin' it to six. One thing, though; I ain't give 'em any repairs. If I'd had a six-dollar family in there I'd had to fixed the window-glass and cleaned out the cistern and mended the roof. It about evens itself up."

"Yes," says Silas, agreeful, "I guess it does. Well, they can have some boxes to burn, out of the store. I'll take 'em on my list. *You* can't go givin' 'em truck, Timothy. If you do, they'll come down on to you for repairs. Now the Ricker's...."

Abigail Arnold spoke up. "They're awful," she says. "Mis' Ricker ain't fit to wash, and the children just show through. Ab's arm won't let him work all winter."

"You take him, Silas," says Timothy. "He's your own employee."

Silas shakes his head. "He's been chasin' me for damages ever since he got hurt," he says.

"Ain't he goin' to get any, Silas?" says Mis' Toplady, pitiful.

"Get any?" says Silas. "It was his own fault. He told me a week before about them belts bein' wore. I told him to lay off till I could fix 'em. But no—he kep' right on. Said his wife was sick and his bills was eatin' him up. He ain't nobody to blame but his own carelessness. I told him to lay off."

I looked over to Mis' Toplady, and she looked over to me. And I looked at Abigail and at Mis' Holcomb, and we all looked at each other. Only Mis' Sykes—she set there listening and looking like her life was just elegant.

"Can't you take that case, Mis' Toplady?" says Silas.

"I'll go and see them *folks*," she says, troubled. And I guess us ladies felt troubled, one and all. And so on during all the while we was discussing the Doles and the Hennings and the Bettses and the rest. And when the meeting was over we four hung around the stove, and Mis' Sykes too.

"I s'pose it's all right," Mis' Toplady says. "I s'pose it is. But I feel like we'd made a nice, new apron to tie on to Friendship Village, and hadn't done a thing about its underclothes."

"I'm sure," says Mis' Sykes, looking hurt for Silas that had cut out the apron, "I'm sure I don't see what you mean. Faith, Hope, and Charity, and the greatest of these is Charity. Does that mean what it says, or don't it?"

"Oh, I s'pose it does," says Mis' Toplady. "But what I think is this: Ain't there things that's greater than the whole three as most folks mean 'em?"

Mis' Sykes, she sort of gasped, in three hitches. "Will you tell me *what*?" she says, as mad as if she'd been faith, hope, and charity personally.

"I dunno ..." says Mis' Toplady, dreamy, "I dunno the name of it. But ladies, it's something. And I can feel it, just as plain as plain."

It was three-four weeks before the new Charity Association got really to running, and had collected in enough clothes and groceries so's we could start distributing. On the day before the next monthly meeting, that was to be in Post-Office Hall again, we started out with the things, so's to make our report to the meeting. Mis' Toplady and I was together, and the first place we went to was Absalom Ricker's. Gertie, Absalom's wife, was washing, and he was turning the wringer with his well hand, and his mother was finishing vests by the stove, and singing a tune that was all on a straight line and quite loud. And the children, one and all, was crying, in their leisure from fighting each other.

"Well," says Mis' Toplady, "how you getting on *now*? Got many washings to do?"

Gertie Ricker, she set down on the wood-box all of a sudden and begun to cry. She was a pretty little woman, but sickly, and with one of them folding spines that don't hold their folks up very good.

"I've got three a week," she says. "I can earn the rent all right."

"I tell her," says Absalom, "if she didn't have no washings, then there'd be something to cry for."

But he said it sort of lack-luster, and like it come a word at a time.

"Do you get out any?" says Mis' Toplady, to improve the topic.

"Out where?" says Gertie. "We ain't no place to go. I went down for the yeast last night."

It kind of come over me: Washing all day and her half sick; Absalom by the stove tending fire and turning wringer; his old mother humming on one note; the children yelling when they wasn't shouting. I thought of their cupboard and I could see what it must hold—cold boiled potatoes and beans, I bet. I thought of their supper-table ... of early mornings before the fire was built. And I see the kind of a life they had.

And then I looked over to the two loaves of bread and the can of fruit and the dozen eggs and the old coat of Timothy's that we'd brought, and it seemed to me these touched the spot of what was the trouble in that house about as much as the smoke that oozed into the room from the chimney. And I glanced over to Mis' Toplady and there she set, with ideas filterin' back of her eyes.

"We've brought you a few things, being you're sick—" she begun, sort of embarrassed; but Absalom, he cut in short, shorter than I ever knew him to speak.

"Who's *we*?" he says.

"Why-a," says Mis' Toplady, stumbling some over her words, "the new society."

Absalom flushed up to the roots of his hair. "What society?" says he, sharp.

Mis' Toplady showed scairt for just a minute, and then she met his eyes brave. "Why," she says, "us—and you. You belong to it. We had it in the paper, and met to the Post-Office Hall the other night. It's for everybody to come to."

"To do what?" says Absalom.

"Why-a," says Mis' Toplady, some put to it, "to—to do nice things for—for each other."

"The town?" says Absalom.

"The town," agrees Mis' Toplady—and pressed ahead almost like she was finding something to explain with. "We meet again to-morrow night," says she. "Couldn't you come—you and Gertie? Come—and mebbe belong?"

Absalom's mad cooled down some. First he looked sheepish and then he showed pleased. "Why, I dunno—could we, Gertie?" he says.

"Is it dress-up?" says Gertie.

"Mercy, no," says Mis' Toplady, "it's every-day. Or not so much so. You'll come, won't you?"

"Mebbe," says Gertie.

When we got outside, I looked at Mis' Toplady, kind of took aback; and it was so that she looked at me.

"Silas'll talk charity his way to that meeting, you know," I says. "I'm afraid he'll hurt Absalom and Gertie. I'm afraid...."

Mis' Toplady looked kind of scairt herself. "I done that before I meant to do it no more'n nothing in this world," she says, "but I dunno—when I begun handin' 'em out stuff I was ashamed to do it without putting it like I done."

"I know," I says, "I know." And know I did. I've give things to poor folks lots of times and glowed up my spine with a virtuous feeling—but something big was always setting somewhere inside me making me feel ashamed of the glow and ashamed of the giving. Who am I that I should be the giver, and somebody else the givee?

We went to the Bettses' and caught Mis' Betts washing up two days' of dishes at four o'clock in the afternoon, and we heard about Joe's losing his job, and we talked to the canary. "We'd ought not to afford him," Mis' Betts says, apologetic. "I always hate to take the money to get him another package of seed—and we ain't much of any crumbs."

And we went to the Haskitts' and found her head tied up with the toothache. Folks looks sick enough with their heads tied up *around*; but when it comes to up and down, with the ends sticking up, they always look like they was going to die. And we went to the Doles' and the Hennings' and carried in the stuff; and one and all them places, leaving things there was like laying a ten-cent piece down on a leper, and bowing to him to help on his recovery. And every single place, as soon as ever we'd laid down the old clothes we'd brought, we invited 'em to join the organization and to come to the meeting next night.

"What's the name of this here club?" Joe Betts asks us.

By that time neither Mis' Toplady nor me would have tied the word "Charity" to that club for anything on earth. We told him we was going to pick the name next night, and told him he must come and help.

"Do come," Mis' Toplady says, and when Mis' Betts hung off: "We're goin' to have a little visiting time—and coffee and sandwiches afterwards," Mis' Toplady adds, calm as her hat. And when we got outside: "I dunno what made me stick on the coffee and the sandwiches," she says, sort of dazed, "but it was so kind of bleak and dead in there, I felt like I just had to say something cheerful and human—like coffee."

"Well," I says, "us ladies can do the refreshments ourselves, so be the rest of the Board stands on its head at the idee of doing 'em itself. *As* I presume likely it will stand."

And this we both of us presumed alike. So on the way home we stopped in to the post-office store and told Silas that we'd been giving out a good many invitations to folks to come to the meeting next night, and mebbe join.

"That's good," says Silas, genial; "that's good. We need the dues."

"We kind of thought coffee and sandwiches to-morrow night, Silas," says Mis' Toplady, experimental, "and a little social time."

"Don't you go to makin' no white-kid-glove doin's out o' this thing," says Silas. "You can't mix up charity and society too free. Charity's religion and society's earthy. And that's two different things."

"Earthy," I says over. "Earthy! So'm I. Ain't it a wonderful word, Silas? Well, us two is going to do the coffee and sandwiches for to-morrow night," I added on, deliberate, determined and serene.

When Silas had done his objecting, and see he couldn't help himself with us willing to solicit the whole refreshments, and when we'd left the store, Mis' Toplady thought of something else: "I dunno," she says, "as we'd ought to leave folks out just because they ain't poor. That," she says, troubled, "don't seem real right. Let's us telephone to them we can think of that didn't come to the last meeting."

So we invited in the telephone population, just the same as them that didn't have one.

The next night us ladies got down to the hall early to do the finishing touches. And on Daphne Street, on my way down, I met Bess Bones again, kind of creeping along. She'd stopped to pat the nose of a horse standing patient, hitched outside the barber-shop saloon—- I've seen Bess go down Daphne Street on market-days patting the nose of every horse one after another.

"Hello, Mis' Marsh," Bess says. "Are you comin' down with another meeting?"

"Yes, sir, Bess," I says, "I am." And then a thought struck me. "Bess," I says—able now to hold up my head like my skull intended, because I felt I could ask her—"you come on up, too—you're invited to-night. Everybody is."

Her face lit up, like putting the curtain up.

"Honest, can I?" she says. "I'd love to go to a meeting again—I've looked in the window at 'em a dozen times. I'll get my bread and be right up."

I tell you, Post-Office Hall looked nice. We'd got in a few rugs and plants, and the refreshment table stood acrost one corner, with a screen around the gas-plate, and the cups all piled shiny and the sandwiches covered with white fringed napkins. And about seven o'clock in come three pieces of the Friendship Village Stonehenge Band we'd got to give their services, and they begun tuning up, festive. And us ladies stood around with our hands under our white aprons; and you'd have thought it was some nice, human doings instead of just duty.

Before much of anybody else had got there, in come them we'd invited first: Absalom Ricker and Gertie, her looking real nice with a new-ironed bow to her neck, and him brushed up in Timothy's old coat and his hair trained to a high peak. And the Bettses—Joe with his beard expected to cover up where there wasn't a necktie and her pretending the hall was chilly so's to keep her cloak on over whatever wasn't underneath. And the Haskitts, him snapping and snarling at her, and her trying to hush him up by agreeing with him promiscuous. And Mis' Henning that her husband didn't show up. We heard afterwards he was down in the barber-shop saloon, dressed up to come but backed out after. And most everybody else come—not only the original 'leven, but some of the telephone folks, and some that the refreshment-bait always catches.

Silas come in late—he'd had to wait and distribute the mail—and when he see the Rickers and the rest of them, he come tearing over to us women in the refreshment corner.

"My dum!" he says, "look at them folks setting down there—Rickerses and Henningses and Bettses and them—how we goin' to manage with them here? The idear of their coming to the meeting!"

"Ain't it some their meeting, Silas?" I says. "The whole society was formed on their account. Seems to me they've got a right—just like in real United States Congress doings."

"But, my dum, woman," says Silas, "how we going to take up their cases and talk 'em over with them setting there, taking it all in? Ain't you got no delicacy to you?" he ends up, ready to burst.

And of course, when you come to think of it, Congress always does do its real business in committees, private and delicate.

Mis' Toplady was ready for Silas.

"You're right about it," she says. "We can't do that, can we? Suppose we don't do so very much business to-night? Let's set some other talk goin'. We thought mebbe—do you s'pose your niece would sing for us, Silas?"

"Mebbe," says Silas, some mollified, through being proud to sinning of his visiting niece; "but I don't like this here—" he was going on.

"Ask her," says Mis' Toplady. "She'll do it for you, Silas."

And Silas done so, ignorant as the dead that he'd been right down managed. Then he went up stage and rapped to begin.

Well, of course I had to read the minutes, being secretary so, and I was ready, having set up half the night before to make them out. And of course, the job was some delicate; but I'd fixed them up what I thought was real nice and impersonal. Like this:

"A meeting of citizens of Friendship Village was held, ———, in Post-Office Hall, for the purpose of organizing a society to do nice things for folks. (Then I give the names of the officers.) Several plans was thought over for making presents to others and for distributing the same. Several families was thought of for membership. It was voted to have two kinds of members, honorary and active. The active pay all the dues and provide the presents, but everybody contributes what they can and will, whether work or similar. A number of ways was thought of for going to work. Things that had ought to be done was talked over. It was decided to hold monthly meetings. Meeting adjourned."

That seemed to me to cover everything real neat, nobody ever paying much attention to the minutes anyway. I suppose that's why they give 'em such a small, stingy name. And when Silas got to reports of committees, Mis' Toplady was no less ready for him. She hopped right up to say that the work that had been put in her hands was all finished, the same as was ordered, and no more to be said about it. And when it come to Unfinished Business, there was me on my feet again to say that the work that had been put in my hands wasn't finished and there'd be more to be said about it later.

Then Silas asked for New Business, and there was a pause. And all of a sudden Absalom Ricker got on to his feet with his arm still in its sling.

"Mr. President," he says, so nice and dignified. And when Silas had done his nod, Absalom went on in his soft, unstarched voice: "It's a real nice idear," he says, "to get up this here club. I for one feel real glad it's going. You ain't got up any line around it. Nobody has to be any one thing in order to get in on it. I've thought for a long time there'd ought to be some place where folks could go that didn't believe alike, nor vote alike, nor get paid alike. I'm glad I come out—I guess we all are. Now the purpose of this here club, as I understand it, is to do nice things for folks. Well, I've got a nice thing to propose for us to do. I'll pitch in and help, and I guess some of the rest of us will. Soon as it comes warm weather, we could get a-hold of that elegant galvanized iron swill-wagon that ain't in use and drive it around the town to do what it's for. Us that don't have work so awful steady could do it, nice as a mice. I dunno whether that comes inside what the club was intended for, but it would be doing a kind of a nice thing for folks, my way of thinking."

Up hopped Eppleby Holcomb—Eppleby being one of those prophet men that can see faint signs sticking up their heads where there ain't much of anything showing.

"That's the ticket, Mr. President," says he. "Us that don't have horses or chickens can sense that all right. If Absalom moves it, I second it."

"Will you help drive it around, Betts?" says Absalom. "Hank Haskitt? Ben Dole? We're all of us home a good deal of the time—we could keep it goin', amongst us. All right," says he, when the men had nodded matter-of-course nods, "sure I make it a motion."

Silas put the motion, looking some dazed. And when it carried, hearty, us ladies sitting over by the refreshment table, and that had bought the wagon, we all burst out and spatted our hands. We couldn't help it. And everybody kind of turned around and passed some remark—and it made a real nice minute.

Then Silas spoke up from the chair kind of sour—being in the Council so, that wouldn't run the wagon.

"The thing's in the city tool-house now," says he, "and it's a good deal in the way where it is. It had ought to be put somewheres."

Up pipes Ben Dole, kind of important and eager, and forgot to address the chair till he was half through, and then done so and ducked and flushed and went on anyhow. And the purport of his remarks was, that he could set that tank in the barn of his lot, that he didn't have no horse for and no use of, and keep it there till spring. And I seconded what he meant, and it got itself carried, and Ben set down like he'd done a thing, same as he had done.

Then, when Silas said what was the next pleasure of the meeting, Mis' Toplady mentioned that they needed carpet rags to make up some rugs for two-three places, and who could give some and help sew them? Mis' Sykes said she could, and Mame and Abigail and me and some more offered up, and Mis' Toplady wrote our names down, and, "How about you, Gertie?" says she to Gertie Ricker.

Gertie looked scairt for a minute, and then my heart jumped pleasant in its socket, *for I see Absalom nudge her*. Yes, sir, he nudged her to say she would, and all of a sudden I knew that he wanted his wife to be taking some part like the rest was; and she says, faint, "I guess so." And when Mis' Sykes asked round, Mis' Haskitt and Mis' Henning said they didn't have much of any rags, but they could come and help sew the rags of them that did have.

"So do," says Mis' Toplady, hearty, "and we'll meet to my house next Tuesday at two o'clock, sha'n't we? And have a cup o' tea."

"What else is the pleasure of the meeting?" says Silas, balancing on his toes as chairman-like as he knew how.

Then on the second row from the back, who should we see getting up but Bess Bones. I hadn't seen her come in and I'd forgot all about her. Her hat was on one side, and the plume that was broke in the middle was hanging idle, not doing any decorating; and I could see the other ladies thinking with one brain that ten to one she'd been drinking, and would break out singing in our very midst. But she hadn't nor she didn't. Only what she said went over the room shrill, as her singing voice was.

"For the land's sakes," says Bess, "if you're goin' to hold protracted meetin's in this hall, why don't you clean up the floor? I never see such a hole. I motion I come in an' scrub it up. I ain't no thousand dollars to subscribe, but a cake o' soap'll keep you from stickin' to the boards."

"Second the motion!" says I, all over me.

And even Silas broke down and smiled like he don't think no president had ought to do. And everybody else kind of laughed and looked at each other and felt the kind of a feeling that don't run around among folks any too often. And when Silas put the motion, kind of grudging, we all voted for it abundant. And Bess set there showing pleased, like an empty room that has had a piece of furniture got for it.

I dunno what it was that minute done to us all. I've often wondered since, what it was. But somehow everybody kind of felt that they all knew something each other knew, only they couldn't rightly name it. Ab and Joe Betts, Mame Holcomb and Eppleby, Gertie and Mis' Toplady and me—we all felt it. Everybody did, unless it was Silas and Mis' Sykes. Silas didn't sense nothing much but that he hoped the meeting was going to run smooth, and Mis' Sykes—well, right in the middle of that glowing minute I see her catch sight of Mame Holcomb's new red waist and she set there thinking of nothing *but* waist either with eyes or with mind.

But the rest of us was sharing a big minute. And I liked us all to be feeling that way—I ain't never liked anything better, without it's the Christmas feeling or the Thanksgiving feeling. And this feeling was sort of like all two. And I betted if only we could make it last—Absalom wouldn't be getting done out of his arm's money-value by Silas, nor the Bettses out of their decent roof by Timothy, nor they wouldn't be no club formed to dole out charity stuff, but we would all know a better way. And things would be different. Different.

I leaned clear past three chairs and nudged Mis' Toplady. She looked round, and I see she was just wiping her eyes on her apron-string—Mis' Toplady never can find her handkerchief when she most wants to cry. And I never said a word—I didn't need to—but we nodded and we both knew what we both knew: that there was a bigger thing in the room that minute than ever Silas knew or guessed when he planned out his plan. And it was what Mis' Toplady had meant when she told him there was something "greater than these"—as most folks mean 'em.

I didn't lose the feeling through the piece by the band that come next, nor through the selection by Silas's niece. The music really made the feeling more so—the music, and our all setting there hearing it together, and everybody in the room being givers, and nobody givees. But when the music stopped, and while I was still feeling all glorified up, what did Mis' Sykes do but break in, something like throwing a stone through a window.

"I should think we might as well get the club name settled to-night," she says with her little formal pucker. "Ain't the Charity Club that we spoke of real nice and dignified for our title?"

It was Mis' Toplady that exploded. It just bare happened it wasn't me, but it turned out to be her.

"Land, land," she says, "*no*! Not one person in fifteen hundred knows what charity means anyhow, and everybody'd get the wrong idee. Let's call it just its plain natural name: The Friendship Village Club. Or, The Whole World Club. Or I dunno but The Universe Club!"

I knew I wouldn't have the sense to keep still right through things. I never do have.

"No, sir!" I says out, "oh, no sir! Universe Club ain't big enough. For if they is any other universe anywhere maybe that might feel left out."

Long before we had settled on any one name, I remember Mis' Toplady come out from behind the refreshments screen and says: "Mr. President, the coffee and sandwiches has come to a boil. Can't you peter off the meeting and adjourn it for one week?"

Which wasn't just exactly how she meant to say it. But it seemed to come in so pat that everybody rustled, spontaneous, in spite of themselves. And us ladies begun passing the plates.

After they'd all gone, we was picking up the dishes when Silas come in to see to the stoves.

"Oh, Silas," I says, "wasn't it a splendid meeting? Wasn't it?"

Silas was pinching, gingerish, at the hot stove-door handle, rather than take his coat-tail for a holder.

"I s'pose *you're* satisfied," he says. "You fed 'em, even if we didn't get much done."

"Not get much done!" I says—"not get much done! Oh, Silas, what more did you want to do than we see done here to-night?"

"Well, what kind of a *charity* meeting was that?" says he, sour and bitter rolled into one.

I went up to him with all of Mis' Toplady's fringed tea-napkins in my hands that it was going to take her most of the next day to do up.

"Why, Silas," I says, "I dunno if it was any kind of a charity meeting. But it was a town meeting. It was a folks' meeting. It was a human meeting. Can't you sense it? Can't you sense it, Silas?" I put it to him: "We got something else besides charity going here to-night—as sure as the living sun."

"I like to know what?" he snaps back, and slammed the stove door.

Mis' Toplady, she looked at him tranquil over the tops of her two pairs of spectacles.

"Something that's in folks," says she—and went on hunting up her spoons.

THE TIME HAS COME

WHEN the minister's wife sent for me that day, it was a real bad time, because I'd been doing up my tomato preserves and I'd stood on my feet till they was ready to come off. But as soon as I got the last crock filled, I changed my dress and pushed my hair up under my hat and thought I'd remember to keep my old shoes underneath my skirt.

The minister's parlor is real cool and shady—she keeps it shut up all day, and it kind of smells of its rose jar and its silk cushions and the dried grasses in the grate; and I sank down in the horse-hair patent rocker, and was glad of the rest. But I kept wondering what on earth the minister's wife could want of me. It wasn't the season for missionary barrels or lumberman's literature—the season for them is house-cleaning time when we don't know what all to do with the truck, and we take that way of getting rid of it and, same time, providing a nice little self-indulgence for our consciences. But this was the dead of Summer, and everybody sunk deep in preserves and vacations and getting their social indebtedness paid off and there wasn't anything going around to be dutiful about for, say, a month or six weeks yet, when the Fall woke up, and the town begun to get out the children's school-clothes and hunt 'em for moths.

"Well, Calliope," says the minister's wife, "I s'pose you wonder what I've got important to say to you."

"True," says I, "I do. But my feet ache so," I says graceful, "I'm perfectly contented to set and listen to it, no matter what it is."

She scraped her chair a little nearer—she was a dear, fat woman, that her breathing showed through her abundance. She had on a clean, starched wrapper, too short for anything but home wear, and long-sleeved cotton under-wear that was always coming down over her hands, in July or August, and making you feel what a grand thing it is to be shed of them—I don't know of anything whatever that makes anybody seem older than to see long, cotton undersleeves on them and the thermometer 90° at the City Bank corner.

"Well," says she, "Calliope, the Reverend and I—" she always called her husband the Reverend—"has been visiting in the City, as you know. And while there we had the privilege of attending the Church of the Divine Life."

"Yes," says I, wondering what was coming.

"Never," says she, impressive, "never have I seen religion at so high an ebb. It was magnificent. From gallery to the back seat the pews were filled with attentive, intelligent people. Outside, the two sides of the street were lined with their automobiles. And this not one Sunday, but every Sunday. It was the most positive proof of the interest of the human heart in—in divine things. It was grand."

"Well, well," says I, following her.

"Now," she says, "the sermon wasn't much. Good, but not much. And the singing—well, Lavvy Whitmore can do just as good when she sets about it. *Then what made folks go?* The Reverend and I talked it over. And we've decided it isn't because they're any better than the village folks. No, they've simply got in the habit of it, they see everybody else going, and they go. And it give us an idea."

"What was that?" says I, encouraging, for I never see where she was driving on at.

"The same situation can be brought about in Friendship Village," says she. "If only everybody sees everybody going to church, everybody else will go!"

I sat trying to figger that out. "Do you think so?" says I, meantime.

"I am sure so," she replies, firm. "The question is, How shall we get everybody to go, till the example becomes fixed?"

"How, indeed?" says I, helpless, wondering which of the three everybodys she was thinking of starting in on.

"Now," she continues, "we have talked it over, the Reverend and I, and we have decided that you're the one to help us. We want you to help us think up ways to get this whole village into church for, say, four Sundays or so, hand-running."

I was trying to see which end to take hold of.

"Well-a," I says, "into which church?"

The minister's wife stared at me.

"Why, ours!" says she.

"Why into ours?" I ask' her, thoughtful.

"My goodness," says she, "what do you s'pose we're in our church for, anyway?"

"I'm sure," says I, "I don't know. I often wonder. I'm in our particular one because my father was janitor of it when I was a little girl. Why are you in it?"

She looked at me perfectly withering.

"I," she says cold, "was brought up in it. There was never any question what one I should be in."

"Exactly," says I, nodding. "And your husband—why is he in our special church?"

"My dear Calliope," says she, regal, "he was *born* in it. His father was minister of it——"

"Exactly," I says again. "Then there's Mame Holcomb, her mother sung in our choir, so she joined ours. And Mis' Toplady, they lived within half a mile of ours out in the country, and the other churches were on the other side of the hill. So they joined ours. And the Sykeses, they joined ours when they lived in Kingsford, because there wasn't any other denomination there. But the rest of the congregation, I don't happen to know what their reasons was. I suppose they was equally spiritual."

The minister's wife bent over toward me.

"Calliope Marsh," says she, "you talk like an atheist."

"Never mind me," I says. "Go on about the plan. Everybody is to be got into our church for a few Sundays, as I understand it. What you going to give them when you get them there?"

She looked at me kind of horror-struck.

"Calliope," says she, "what has come over you? The Reverend is going to preach, of course."

"About what?" says I, grim. "Describin' the temple, and telling how many courts it had? Or giving us a little something exegitical—whatever that means?"

For a minute I thought she was going to cry, and I melted myself. If I hadn't been preserving all the morning, I wouldn't never have spoke so frank.

"Honest," I says, "I don't know what exegitical does mean, but I didn't intend it insulting. But tell me this—just as truthful as if you wasn't a minister's wife: Do you see any living, human thing in our church service here in the village that would make a living, human young folk really want to go to it?"

"They'd ought to want to go to it," says she.

"Never mind what they'd ought to want," says I, "though I ain't so clear they'd ought to want it, myself. Just as truthful as if you wasn't a minister's wife—do you?"

"No," says she, "but——"

"Now," I says, "you've said it. And what is true for young is often true for old. If you want to meet that, I'm ready to help you. But if you just want to fill our church up full of folks, I don't care whether it's full or not—not that way."

"Well," she says, "I'm sure I only meant what was for the best in my husband's work——"

I put out my hand to her. All of a sudden, I saw her as she was, doing her level best inside the four walls of her—and I says to myself that I'd been a brute and, though I was glad of it, I'd make up for it by getting after the thing laying there underneath all the words.

For Friendship Village, in this particular, wasn't any different from any other village or any other town or city of now. We had fifteen hundred folks and we had three churches, three ministers at Eight Hundred Dollars apiece annually, three cottage organs, three choirs, three Sunday School picnics in Summer, three Sunday School entertainments in Winter, three sets of repairs, carpets, conventions and delegates, and six stoves with the wood to buy to run 'em. And out of the fifteen hundred folks, from forty to sixty went to each church each Sunday. We were like that.

In one respect, though, we differed from every other town. We had Lavvy Whitmore. Lavvy was the town soprano. She sung like a bird incarnate, and we all got her for Sunday School concerts and visiting ministers and special occasions in general. Lavvy didn't belong to any church. She sort of boarded round, and we couldn't pin her down to any one choir.

"For one reason," she said, "I haven't got enough clothes to belong to any one choir. I've been driven distracted too many times looking at the same plaid waist and the same red bird and the same cameo pin in choirs to do it for anybody else. By kind of boarding round the way I do, I can give them all a change."

The young minister over to the White Frame church—young Elbert Kinsman—he took it harder than the rest.

"How are your convictions, Miss Lavvy?" he had once been heard to say.

"My convictions?" she answered him. "They are that there isn't enough difference in the three to be so solemn and so expensive over. Especially the expensive," she added. "Is there now?"

"No," young Elbert Kinsman had unexpectedly replied, "I myself don't think there is. But——"

"The only thing is," Lavvy had put in irreverent, "*you* can't get rid of that 'but,' and I have!"

"You send for Lavvy," I says now to our minister's wife. "She'll think of something."

So there we were, with a kind of revival on our hands to plan before we knew it, because our minister's wife was like that, much more like that than he was. He had a great deal of emphasis, but she had a great deal of force.

Going home that morning, I went a little out of my way and come round by Shepherd's Grove. Shepherd's Grove lays just on the edge of the village, not far from the little grassy triangle in the residence part—and it always rests me to go there. Walking through it that morning I remember I thought:

"Yes, I s'pose this kind of extry effort must be all right—even Nature enters into it real extensive. Every Summer is an extry effort—a real revival, I guess. But oh," I says to myself, wishful, "that's so spontaneous and unanimous! I wish't folks was more like that...."

I was filling in for organist while ours was away on a vacation to her husband's relatives. That sounds so grand and I'd ought to explain that I can only play pieces that are written in the natural. But by picking out judicious, I can get along through the morning and evening services very nice. I don't dare ever attempt prayer-meeting, because then somebody is likely to pipe up and give out a hymn that's in sharps or flats, without thinking. I remember one night, though, when I just had to play for prayer-meeting being the only one present that knew white notes from black. There was a visiting minister. And when he give out his first hymn, I see it was "There is a Calm for Those That Weep" in three flats, and I turned around on the stool, and I says, "Wouldn't you just as lief play the piece on the opposite page? That's wrote natural." He done so, looking some puzzled, and well he might, for the one I mentioned happened to be, "Master, the Tempest is Raging." I was a kind of a limited organist but then I filled in, vacations and such, anyhow. And it was so I was doing that Summer.

And so they left it to me to kind of plan the order of services for them four Sundays in September that they decided on. That was nice to do—I'd been hankering to get my hands on the services many a time. And a night or two afterwards, our minister come down to talk this over with me. I'd been ironing all that blessed day, and just before supper my half bushel of cherries had come down on me, unexpected. I was sitting on the front porch in the cool of the day, pitting them. The sun wasn't down yet, and folks was watering lawns and tinkering with blinds and screens and fences, or walking round pinching off dead leaves; and being out there sort of rested me.

Our minister sat down on the top stoop-step. It had been an awful hot day, and he looked completely tuckered out.

"Hot, ain't it?" says I, sympathetic,—you can sympathize with folks for the weather without seeming to reproach 'em, same as sympathy for being tired out does to 'em.

"Very warm," says he. "I've made," he says, "eleven calls this afternoon."

"Oh, did you?" I says. "What was the occasion of them?"

He looked surprised. "Pastoral calls," he says, explaining.

"Oh," I says. "Sick folks?"

"Why no, no," says he. "My regular rounds. I've made," he adds, "one hundred and fourteen calls this month."

I went on pitting cherries. When I look back on it now, I know that it wasn't natural courage at all that made me say what I did. It was merely the cherries coming on top of the ironing.

"Ain't life odd?" says I. "When *you* go to see folks, it's duty. And when I go to see folks, I do it for a nice, innocent indulgence."

He looked kind of bewildered and sat there fanning himself with the last foreign missionary report and not saying anything for a minute.

"What did you find to talk about with 'em?" I says, casual.

"Well," he said, "I hardly know. The range of interests, I must say, is not very wide. There has been a good deal of sickness in the congregation this Summer——"

"Yes," I says, "I know. Mis' Emmons's limb has been troubling her again. Mis' Temples' headaches have come back. Old Mr. Blackwell has got hold of a new dyspepsia remedy. At the Holmans' the two twins fell into an empty cistern and got scraped. And Grandma Oxner don't see any change in the old complaint. I'm familiar with 'em."

He smiled at that. "They *have* a good many burdens to bear," he says, patient. "But——"

"But," I says, "don't it seem wicked to ask a man to set and listen to everybody's troubles for one hundred and fourteen calls a month, and expect him to feel he's doing the Lord's work?"

"The office of comforter——" he began.

"When," says I, "was complaints ever lessened by dwelling on 'em—tell me that? Oh," I says, "it ain't you I'm blaming, nor the other ministers either. I'm blaming us, that calls a minister to come and help us reveal the word of God to ourselves, and then expect a social call a month, or more, off'n him, once around the congregation—or else be uppish and mebbe leave the church."

"The office of spiritual adviser always demands——" he started in, and concluded it as might have been expected.

"How much religion really, *really*, do they let you talk on these calls?" I ask' him. "Don't it seem kind of bad taste if you say much about it? And as a matter of fact, don't ministers pride themselves nowdays on being all-around men who can talk about everything, from concerts to motion pictures, and this here city gollif? Of course they do. That is, if folks keep off their complaints long enough to leave you prove how really broad your interests are."

"Yes, I know—well," he says patient, "they expect the calls. What," he adds, "had you thought of for the order of the four Sunday services?"

"I thought," I says, "for the first fifteen minutes or so, we might sing together."

"A short praise service," says he, comprehending. "Well—that's a little out of the order for the Sunday morning service, but it might be indulged."

"Yes," I says, dry. "Praise ought not to offend most people. And then I thought of it for what it does to people to sing together for a while. It makes real things seem sort of possible, I always think. After the Doxology, we might start in with 'America,' and——"

"America?" says he.

I waited. I thought the next observation belonged to him.

"We've sung 'America' at Sunday evening mass meetings," he says, "but for the opening hymn of the regular morning worship—still, of course it's in the hymnal. I suppose there is really no objection."

"That," says I, "was how I looked at it. There's no objection. Then the Lord's prayer—all of us together. And the reading—something read from one heart right to another, wouldn't it be? And then we might sing again—'Love For Every Unloved Creature,' or something of that sort. I think," I says, "we'd ought to be very careful what hymns we pick out, for these Sundays. Take just the religious ones, why don't you?"

"I beg your pardon," said our minister. "What did you say then?"

"Well, for instance," I says....

" 'The Son of God goes forth to war
A kingly crown to gain.
His blood-red banner streams afar.
Who follows in his train?'

"I call a good deal of that hymn immoral. Think of that gentle soul caring to gain a kingly crown. Think of his having a blood-red banner. Think of him going forth *to war*. It's a wicked hymn, some of it."

"Oh, well," said our minister, "those things are just figurative. You mustn't take them too literally, Miss Marsh."

I looked over at him, across my cherries.

"We're saying that pretty often these days," I said. "Sometimes it's glorious true and sometimes it's stupid false."

"Well," he says, "that needn't enter into the services for these Sundays. We might of course do well to pick out the hymns with care. What else had you thought of?"

"I thought," I said, "of having the Sunday School come in then and march down the aisle, singing—not 'We Are Little Soldiers,' or anything like that, but 'I Think When I Read That Sweet Story of Old,' say. And then have them repeat something—well," I says, "I found a little verse the other day. I never saw it before—mebbe you have. I've been meaning to ask the superintendent how it would be to have the children learn to say that."

I said it for him:

" 'The year's at the Spring,
The day's at the morn,
Morning's at seven,

The hill-side's dew-pearled.
The lark's on the wing,
The snail's on the thorn,
God's in his heaven,
All's right with the world.'

"And then," I says, "have them add: 'And oh God, help the last line to get to be true for everybody, and help me to help make it true. Amen,' That," I says, "might do for one day. Then you talk to 'em for five minutes. And then dismiss them."

"*Dismiss* them?" he said. "Not have them remain to the service?"

"Why, no," I says, "not unless you can interest and occupy them. Which no sermons do for little children."

"Where would the mothers that are in church *send* their children to?" says he.

"We ought to have the rooms downstairs open," I says, "and have somebody in charge, and have quiet exercises and story-telling and pictures for them."

"My dear Miss Marsh," he says, "that would be a revolution."

"True," says I, serene. "Ain't life odd?" I adds. "One minute we're saying, shocked: 'But that would be a revolution.' And the next minute we're harping away on keeping alive the revolutionary spirit. I wonder which of the two we really mean?"

"Well, then, what else?" says he, pacific.

"Then," I says, "I wish we could have five minutes of silent prayer. And then right off, the sermon—and no hymn after that at all, but let the sermon end with the benediction—a real cry to God to be with us and to live in us. That's all."

I had to go out in the kitchen then to empty a bowl of my pitted fruit, and when I come back the minister stood there, smiling.

"Ah, Miss Marsh," he said, "you've forgotten a very important thing. You've forgotten the collection."

"No," says I. "No, I haven't. Except on the days when it's a real offering for some work for God. I'd take a collection then. The rest of the time I'd have the minister's salary and the fuel and the kerosene paid for by checks, private."

After he'd gone, I set there going over, miserable, the things I'd said to him about the services that it was his job to do. And though I was miserable enough—I honestly couldn't be sorry. You know the difference in them two?

I was to engage Lavvy Whitmore to lead our singing for the four Sundays, and I went over to see her the next afternoon. She was cleaning the lamps when I stepped up to the kitchen door, so I went right in and sat down at the end of the table, and helped her with the chimneys. She was a pretty little thing—little, but with black eyes that mentioned her thoughts before ever any of the rest of her agreed to announce 'em. And plenty of thoughts, too, Lavvy had. She wasn't one of the girls that is turned out by the thousands, that wouldn't recognize their own minds if they was to meet 'em unbeknownst; but one that her mind was cut out, careful, by a pattern part of her own selecting, and not a pattern just laid on to it, haphazard, by the folks that she lived neighbor to, and went with when she went.

"Lavvy," I says, "we want to speak for you to sing to our church the four Sundays in September, when we have special services to get everybody to go, so's everybody'll see everybody else going, and go too. Can we? Will you?"

"I've been spoke for," says she, "by the White Frame church for the four September Sundays. For the same reason."

"Go on!" I says. "Do you mean to tell me that they're going to have a competition revival?"

"Well," she says, "they're going to make an extra effort to get folks out for the four Sundays."

"Copied it off'n us," I says thoughtful. "Well, I guess the four Sundays can't be regularly copyrighted by us, can they? But I thought their minister didn't like revivals?" I says.

"Oh, he don't—Elbert Kinsman don't," says Lavvy. "It's the rest of 'em wants it. He told me he thought it was a mistake."

"That young Elbert Kinsman," I says, "he loves *folks*. I saw it in his face long ago."

Lavvy went on trimming wicks.

"And then the Red Brick church," says she, "*they've* spoke for me to sing for them for the four Sundays in September too."

"Land of life," I says, "they haven't! What on earth have they done that for?"

"Oh," says Lavvy, "to get everybody to go, so's everybody'll see everybody else going, and———"

"Don't, Lavvy," I says. "That makes me feel kind of sick."

"So it done to me," she says. "And I'll tell you the same as I told them: No, I won't sing those four Sundays. I ain't going to be here. I don't know yet where I'm going, but I'll go off somewheres—where things are better—if I have to go blackberrying in Shepherd's Grove."

"My land," I says, "I've a great good notion to get my pail and go along with you."

We talked about it quite a while that afternoon, Lavvy and me. And though all along I'd been feeling sort of sore and sick over the whole idea—and I might have known that I was, by the chip-shouldered way I had talked to our minister—still, it wasn't till there by the lamps that I come to a realization of myself, and of some other things just as foolish, and that I faced around and begun to ask myself, plain, what in the world was what.

For it was as true as possible: As soon as it got out around that our church was laying plans for a revival—not an evangelist revival, but a home-made one—it had happened just as might have been expected. The other two churches was afraid we'd get their folks away from them, and they says they'd make an extra effort to get folks out, as well. They fell into the same hope—to "fill up" the churches, and see if we couldn't get folks started attending regular. Somebody suggested having a month's union services in each of the three churches, but they voted that three months of this would get monotonous, while the novelty of the other way would "get folks out."

No sooner had we all settled on that, then we slipped, by the gradualest degrees, into the next step, that was as inevitable as two coming after one. We begun being secret about what we meant to have, not telling what the order of exercises was going to be, or what special music we was getting up. And then come along the next thing, as regular as three coming after two—we begun sort of running one another to see who could get the most folks. At first we sent out printed invitations addressed to likely spots; then we took to calling to houses by committees, and delivering invitations in person. Now and then rival visiting committees would accidentally meet to the same house and each try to out-set the other. And from this, one or two things developed, as things will, that made a little uppishness here and there. For out of certain situations, uppishness does seem to arise, same as cream out of milk, or dust out of furniture.

One afternoon I looked out my window, and I see the three Sunday school superintendents come marching up my brick walk—ain't it funny how, when men goes out with a proposition for raising pew-rent, or buying a new furnace for the manse, or helping along the town, they always go two or three strong? If you notice, they do.

"Come right in, gentlemen," I says. "If it's money, I can't give you a cent. If it's work, I'm drove to death as it is. But if it's advice, I do enjoy myself giving that."

It was our own superintendent that spoke, as being the least foreign to me, I s'pose,—though it happened that I was better acquainted with both the other two.

"It's neither, Miss Marsh," he says, "it's some ideas we want off'n you. We've got," says he, "a plan."

Then he unrolled it, assisted by the other two.

"We thought," he says, "that in all this added interest in church attendance which we are hoping to stimulate, the three churches had ought to pull together a little."

At that my heart jumped up. It was what I had been longing for, and grieving because it didn't come true.

"We thought we'd ought to have a little more community effort," says the White Frame superintendent, clearing his throat. I guess he knew how that word "community" always gets me. I'd rather read that one word than half the whole books on the market.

"Oh, yes," I says. "Yes! I think so too."

"We thought we'd ought to make the experience one of particular blessing and fellowship," says the Red Brick superintendent, fairly beaming.

And me, the simple soul, I beamed back.

"Count on me," says I, fervent, "to do anything in the world to help on a thing like that!"

"We were sure of it," said our superintendent, "and that is why we have come to you. Now," says he, "the idea is this: We thought we'd each take a color—give each church a color, you know."

"A color?" says I.

"Exactly," says he. "The White Frames white. The Red Bricks red. And us blue. Then on each of the four Sundays the number present in the three churches will be kept track of and totaled at the end of the month. And, at the end of the month, the church having had the largest attendance for the whole time shall be given a banquet by the other two. What do you say to that?"

What did I say to that? Somehow I got them out of the house, telling them I'd send them word later. When I feel as deep as I did then, I know I can't do justice, by just thoughts or just words, to what I mean inside. So I let the men go off the best I could. And then I went back into my sitting room, with the August sun pouring in all acrost the air like some kind of glory that we didn't understand; and I set down in it, and thought. And the thing that come to me was them early days, them first days when the first Christians were trying to plan ways that they could meet, and hoping and longing to be together, and finding caves and wild places where they could gather in safety and talk about their wonderful new knowledge of the fatherhood of God and the brotherhood of man, and the divine experience of the spirit, here and after. And then I thought of this red, white and blue denominational banquet. Oh, what a travesty it was even on the union that the three colors stand for. And I thought of our talk about "getting people out," and "filling up the churches," and I thought of the one hundred and fourteen or more social calls that we require a month from our pastors. And I says to myself:

"Oh, Calliope Marsh, has it come to this—*has* it? Is it like this only in Friendship Village? Or is it like this out in the world too? And, either way, what are we going to do about it?"

There was one thing I could do about it. I went to see our minister and his wife, and I told 'em firm that I couldn't have anything more to do about the extra September services, and that they would have to get somebody else to play the organ for all four Sundays. They was both grieved—and I hated to hurt them. That's the worst about being true to something you believe—it so often hurts somebody else. But there wasn't any other way to do.

"But Miss Marsh," says our minister, "don't you see that it is going to be a time of awakening if we all stand by each other and support the meetings?"

"Support the meetings!" I wondered how many times, in those first days, they had to argue that. But I didn't say anything—I just sat still and ached.

"But Miss Marsh," said the minister's wife, "we have so depended on you. And your influence—what about that?"

"I can't help it," I says—and couldn't say no more.

Mis' Postmaster Sykes was there, and *she* piped up:

"But it's so *dig*nified, Calliope," she says. "No soliciting, no pledging people to be present, no money-begging for expenses. No anything except giving people to understand that not attending ain't real respectable."

It was them words that give me the strength to get up and go home without breaking down. And all the way up Daphne Street I went saying it over: "No anything except giving people to understand not attending ain't real respectable. No, not anything only just that."

Near my own gate I come on young Elbert Kinsman, minister of the White Frame church, going along alone.

"Oh, Mr. Kinsman," I burst out unbeknownst, "*can* you imagine Jesus of Nazareth belonging to a denomination?"

All of a sudden, that young minister reached out and took my hand.

"He loved men," he said only, "and he was very patient with them."

And then I went into my dark house, with some other words ringing in my ears: "Lighten mine eyes—lighten mine eyes, lest I sleep the sleep of the dead."

But oh, that first September Sabbath morning. It was one of them days that is still all deep Summer, but with just a little light mantel of Autumn—more like a lace boa than a mantel, though—thrown round over things. It was Summer by the leaves, by the air it was Summer, by the gay gardens and the face of the sky; and yet somewhere, hiding inside, was a little hint of yellow, a look of brown, a smell in the wind maybe—that let you know it was something else besides. It wasn't that the time was any less Summer. It was just that it was Summer and a little Autumn too. But I always say that you can't think Autumn without thinking Winter; and you can't think Winter without thinking Spring; and Spring and Summer are not really two, but just one. And so there you have the whole year made one and nothing divided.... What if God were intelligence and spirit harmonized and made one? What if all that is the matter with us is just that we intelligences and spirits have not yet been harmonized and made one?

I've got a little old piano that the keys rattle, and Sunday mornings, for years now, I always go to that after breakfast, and sit down in my apron, and play some anthems that I remember: "As Pants the Hart," and "Glory Be to God in the Highest," and like that. I did it that first Autumn Sunday morning, with my windows open and the muslin curtains blowing and the sun slanting in, and a little smell of wild mint from the bed by the gate. And I knew all over me that it was Sunday morning—I'd have known it no matter if I hadn't known.

For all I took as long as I could doing my dishes and brushing up the floor and making my bed and feeding my chickens, it was only half past nine when I was all through. Then I got my vegetables ready for dinner, and made me a little dessert, and still it was not quite ten o'clock. So then I give it up and went in, and sat down where I could see them go past to church. I had wanted to keep busy till after half past ten, when they'd all be in their pews.

Already they were going by, folks from up the street and round the corner: some that didn't usually go and that I couldn't tell which of the churches they'd be going to, and I wondered how they could tell themselves; and then some that sat near me in church, and that I usually walked along with.

"No," I thought, "no such nonsense as this for me. Ever. Nor no red, white and blue banquet, either."

Then, all of a sudden, the first bells began to ring. All the little churches in the village have bells and steeples—they were in debt for them for years. But the bells ... all my life long I'd been hearing them rung Sunday morning. All my life I had answered to them—to our special one because, as I said, my father had been janitor there, and he had rung the bell; but just the same, I had answered, always. The bells had meant something to me. They meant something now. I loved to hear them. Pretty soon they stopped, and there was just the tramp of feet on the board walk. I sat there where I was, without moving, the quarter of an hour until the bells began again. And when the bells began again it seemed as if they rang right there in the room with me, but soft and distant too,—from a long way off where I wasn't any more. Always it had been then, at the second bell, that mother had stood in the hall and asked me if I was ready.... I sat there where I was, the quarter of an hour until the bells began again, and I knew this was the last bell, that would end in the five strokes—rung slow, and that when they stopped, all the organs would begin together. And then I could have cried aloud the thing that had been going in me and through me since the first bell had begun to ring:

"Oh, God. It's the invisible church of the living God—it's the place that has grown out of the relation of men to you, out of the striving of men to find you, and out of their longing to draw together in search of you. It is our invisible church from the old time. Why then—when men read things into the visible church that never belonged there, when there has crept into and clung there much that is false, why is it that we who know this must be the ones to withdraw? It is your church and the church of all those who try to know you. What shall we do to make it whole?"

Before I knew what I was doing, I was slipping my long cloak on over my work-dress, and then I was out on the street. And I remember that as I went, the thing that kept pouring through my mind was that I wasn't the only one. But that all over, in other towns at that very hour, there were those whose hearts were aching as mine had ached, and who had nowhere to go. I don't know yet what I meant to do; but over and over in my head the words kept going:

"What shall we *do* to make it whole?"

The last bell had stopped when I came to the little grassy triangle where the three churches faced. And usually, on Sunday mornings, by the time the last bell has rung, the triangle is still except for a few hurrying late-comers. But now, when I turned the corner and faced it, I saw people everywhere. Before each little church the steps, the side-walk, and out in the street, were thronged with people, and people were flowing out into the open spaces. And in a minute I sensed it: There wasn't room. There wasn't room—for there were fifteen hundred people living in Friendship Village, and all the little churches of the town together wouldn't hold that many, nor even as many of them as were assembled there that day. But instead of thinking what to do, and how not to waste the time when so many had got together, all that kept going through my head was those same words that I had been saying:

"What shall we *do* to make it whole?"

And yet those words were what made me think what to do. On the steps of our church I saw our superintendent, looking wild and worried, and I ran right up to him, and I said two words. And in a minute those two words went round, and they spoke them in the crowd, and they announced them inside our church, and somebody went with those words to the other churches. And then we were all moving out and along together to where the two words pointed us: Shepherd's Grove.

There's a rough old bandstand in Shepherd's Grove where once, long ago, the German band used to give evening concerts. The bandstand had nearly fallen to pieces, but it was large enough. The three ministers went up there together, and round the base of the bandstand came gathering the three choirs, and in a minute or two there we all were under the trees of the Grove, the common trees, that made a home for us all, on the common earth, under the common sky.

"Praise God from whom all blessings flow" came first, because it said the thing that was in the hearts of us all. And then we wondered what would be, because of the three separate sermons up there before us, all prepared, careful, by three separate ministers, in three separate manses, for three separate congregations. But the thing seemed to settle itself. For it was young Elbert Kinsman who rose, and he didn't have any prepared sermon in his hands. His hands were empty when he stretched them out toward us. And he said:

"My friends and fellow-lovers of God, and seekers for his law in our common life, this is for me an end and a beginning. As I live, it is for me the end of the thing that long has irked me, that irks us all, that we are clinging to nobody can tell why, or of whose will. I mean the division of unreason in the household of love. For me the folly and the waste and the loss of efficiency of denominationalism have forever ceased. In this hour begins for me a new day: The day when I stand with all men who strive to know God, and call myself by no name save the name which we all bear: Children of the Father, and brothers to Man."

I don't know what else he said—I heard, but I heard it in something that wasn't words, but that was nearer, and closer up to, and clearer in my ears than any words. And I knew that what he was saying had been sounding in my heart for long; and that I had heard it trying to speak from the hearts of others; and that it wasn't only in Friendship Village, but it was all over the world that people are ready and waiting for the coming of the way that had been shown to us that day. Who knows how it will come at last,—or what form it will take? But we do know that the breaking down of the meaningless barriers must come first.

When the young minister had finished, we stood for a moment in silent prayer. You can *not* stand still in the woods and empty out your own will, without prayer being there instead, quiet, like love.

Then all together, and as if a good many of us had thought of it first, we began to sing:

"There's a wideness in God's loving
Like the wideness of the sea...."

No sooner had we begun than deep in the wood, clear and sweet above the other singing, there came a voice that we all knew. It was Lavvy—I stood where I could see her coming. She was in a cotton dress, and she had done as she had said—gone into the wood—"where better things are." And there we had come to find them too. She came down the green aisles, singing; and we were all singing—I wish I might have been where I could hear that singing mount. But I was, and we all were, where we could look into one another's hearts and read there the common longing to draw near unto God. And the great common God was in our midst.

THE FACE OF FRIENDSHIP VILLAGE

THE day that they denominated Threat Hubbelthwait for mayor of Friendship Village was band-concert night. It's real back-aching work to go to our band concerts, because we ain't no seats—nothing but a bandstand in the middle of the market square; but yet we all of us do go, because it's something to do. And you die—you *die* for some place to go to see folks and to move around among them, elbow near.

I was resting on the bottom step of the bandstand between tunes, when Mis' Timothy Toplady come by.

"Hold up your head," says she. "You're going to be mayored over in a minute by a man that ain't been drunk for six months. I dunno but they used that in the campaign. This town ain't got a politic to its name."

"Do they know yet," I ask' her, "who's going to run against him?"

"I heard 'Lish Warren," says Mis' Toplady. "They want Eppleby to run interdependent, but he won't leave himself down to run against Threat and 'Lish, I don't believe. I wish't," Mis' Toplady says, "I was men."

But all of a sudden she sort of straightened up there to the foot of the bandstand.

"No, I don't," she says. "I wish't I was a human being. A human being like the Lord meant me to be, with a finger in His big pie as well as in Timothy Toplady's everlasting apple-pie. I wish't—oh, I wish't I was a real human being, with my brains in my head instead of baked into pies and stitched into clothes and used to clean up floors with."

I've often wished that, too, and every woman had ought to. But Mis' Toplady had ought to wish it special. She's big and strong of limb, and she can lift and carry and put through, capable and swift. She's like a woman left from some time of the world when women was some human-beinger than they are now, and she's like looking ahead a thousand years.

"But just *half* a human," she says now, dreamy, "would know that election day ought to be differn't from the run o' days. Some men votes," she says, "like they used the same muscles for votin' that they use for bettin' and buyin' and sellin'. I wonder if they do."

When the band started to play, we moved over towards the sidewalk. And there we come on Timothy Toplady and Silas and Mis' Sykes and Eppleby Holcomb and Mame, and two-three more. We stood there together, listening to the nice, fast tune. They must have been above six-seven hundred folks around the square, all standing quiet in the rings of the arc lights or in the swinging shadows, listening too.

The market square is a wonderful, big open place to have in the middle of a town. It had got set aside years ago to be a park some day, and while it was a-waiting for parkhood, the town used the edge of it for a market and wood-yard. It stretched away 'most to the track and the Pump pasture, and on three sides of it Friendship Village lay—that night with stores shut up and most of the houses shut up while folks took their ease—though it *was* a back-aching ease—hearing the nice, fast, late tunes.

Right while we was keeping still, up slouched Threat Hubbelthwait, the new mayor nominee.

"Evenin'," says he, with no reverence for the tune. "Ain't this here my dance?"

"I heard you was up to lead us one," says Mis' Toplady, dry.

Threat took it for congratulations. "Thank you kindly," says he, easy. "It's a great trust you folks are talkin' of placin' in me."

"Oh, 'most everybody in town has been trustin' you for years, ain't they, Threat?" says Mis' Toplady, sweet.

That scairt Timothy, her lawful lord, and he talked fast to cover up, but Threat pretended not to hear anyway, and pretty soon he slouched on. And when the piece was over, and the clapping:

"Mercy," says Mame Holcomb, "the disgrace it'll be to have that man for mayor! How'd he get himself picked out?"

Silas Sykes explained it. "Threat Hubbelthwait," says he, "is the only man in this town that can keep the party in at this election. If Threat don't run, the party's out."

"Why not leave the party *go* out, then?" says Mis' Toplady, innocent.

"Listen at that!" says Silas. "Leave the party go out! What do we belong to the party for if we're willing to leave it go out?"

"What," says Mis' Toplady, troubled, "do you belong to it for if you're willing to leave it stay in along with a bad man?"

"We stand by the party to keep the party from being disrupted, woman," says Silas.

Mis' Toplady looks at him, puzzled.

"Well," she says, "I *have* made an apple-pie to keep the apples from spoiling, but yet that wasn't the real, true purpose of the pie."

Eppleby Holcomb kind of chuckled, and just then we all got jostled for a minute with a lot passing us. Lem Toplady come by, his girl on his arm, and a nice, sheepish grin for his mother. Jimmy Sturgis, Jr., and Hugh Merriman and Mis' Uppers's boy and two-three more of that crowd, with boys' eyes in brown faces, and nice, manly ways to their shoulders. Everybody was walking round between tunes. And everywhere, in and out, under foot, went the children, eight, ten, twelve years apiece to 'em, and couldn't be left home because they wasn't anybody to leave 'em with. And there they was, waiting to be Friendship Village when the rest of us should get out of the market square for good; and there was Friendship Village, over beyond the arc light, waiting to be their town.

"Eppleby," I says, "why don't you run against Threat, and mayor this town like it ought to be?"

"Because," Silas spoke up for him, "Eppleby belongs to the party."

"You *do*?" says I to Eppleby. "Well, if Threat, that would like to see the world run backwards, and you, that's a-pushing some on the west side like the Lord meant—if you two belongs to the same party, I bet the party's about ready to come in two pieces anyhow. Why don't you leave it go, and get denominated on your own hook, Eppleby?" I ask' him.

"I'm going to if 'Lish gets put up," he says low, to me. But out loud he says, careless: "I couldn't beat the saloon folks. They're solid for Threat."

"But ain't we more folks to this town than them?" Mame asks.

"Yes," says Eppleby, "but they don't vote. Half the best men won't touch the city hall with a clothes prop. The business men can't vote much—they've got too mixed a trade, both sides eatin' groceries and wearin' clothes. And election time comes when them out towards the city limits is doing Spring plowin' and won't bother to come in town. (We'd took in most of the surrounding country in our efforts to beat out Red Barns in population.) And the *Evening Daily* was give to understand six months ago that the brewery ad. would come out if Threat wa'n't their ticket. Anybody that runs against him is beat before the polls open."

"Among 'em all, what about the town?" says I.

Mis' Sykes spoke up, majestic. "The town," says she, "is as good as any town. I'm sure we've got as many nice residences and well-kep' yards, and as many modern improvements as most towns our size. *My* part, I'm too patriotic to be all the time askin' for more."

"I wonder, Mis' Sykes," I couldn't help saying, "you ain't too religious ever to pray about yourself."

The band always plays "America" to go home on, not so much out of patriotism, I guess, as to let folks know it's time to go home. And just as they was tuning up, Mis' Toplady leaned over to me, brooding.

"I wouldn't care so much," she says, "if it wasn't Lem's first vote. Lem was twenty-one in the spring, and it's his first vote. I just can't bear to think of his voting for Threat or 'Lish, to cut his voting teeth on."

"I know," I says. "So it is Hugh Merriman's first vote—and Mis' Uppers's boy and Jimmy Sturgis's, Jr. Don't it seem too bad?"

Mis' Toplady looked at the men. "Couldn't you do something to your election day that you own so personal?" she snaps. "Couldn't you make it a day that is a day? A day that would make folks want to vote decent, and be some kitterin'-minded about votin' bad?"

"Like what?" says Timothy, blank.

"Oh—I dunno," says Mis' Toplady, restless. "Somethin' that'll roust folks up and give 'em to see their town like a wagon to be pulled and not one to be rode in. Exercises, mebbe———"

"*Exercises!*" says Silas Sykes, explosive. "You'll be wantin' the stores closed election day, next thing."

"I mean that now," says Mis' Toplady. "Exercises," she went on, "that'll show 'em what's being done for 'em in the world—and the universe—and I dunno but other places. Exercises that'll make 'em think ahead and out, and up and in the air instead of just down into their pocketbooks. I dunno. Exercises that'll make 'em see the state like a state, *their* state———"

"My dum, woman," says Silas, "election day ain't no Fourth of July proceedings."

"Ain't it?" says Mis' Toplady. "That's what I dunno. It kind of seems to me as if it was."

Then the band jabbed into "America" abundant, and the men took off their hats, patriotic as pictures. And I stood there, kind of looking at us all while we listened. I see all them hundreds of us out of the stores and houses of Friendship Village that was laying over behind us there in the dark, waiting for us to keep on a-making it; and I see Lem Toplady and the rest of 'em going to do their first move public towards the making. And while the band was playing and everybody humming their country's air, negligent in their throats, I started to slip off—I couldn't help it—and to go home by the back street, like I didn't want to meet the village face to face.

But I hadn't got very far when the band done a thing it's been doing lately—ever since the new leader come that's some kind of a foreigner up to the round-house. It run off into some kind of a French piece with a wonderful tang to it. The children have been singing it in school, with some different words to it, and when the band begun it now, they all kind of hummed it, all over the square. The Marseilles, I think they call it—like a kind of cloth. When I hear it, it always makes me want to go and start something. It done that now. And I says to myself:

"What you slinkin' off home for, actin' like the 'best' people that can't look their town in the face at election time? Go on down Daphne Street like a citizen, that you are one."

And I did, and walked along the little watching streets with all the rest of us, and that march music in my heels. And listening to it, and seeing us all streaming to our homes, I could 'most have felt like we was real folks living in a real town, like towns was meant to be.

But I lost the feeling two days after, when 'Lish got the other denomination, and begun swaggering around similar to Threat, peddling promises. When 'Lish done that, though, Eppleby done like he said and come out to run interdependent; only he done it real halfhearted, and them that signed his petition was mostly out of business or retired or working for the Government or ministers or like that, and everybody thought they was about the only ones that would be to the polls for him. Because the rest was already engaged in uttering the same old fear that voting for Eppleby now would be throwing their vote away. And they allowed that Threat was a little better than 'Lish, or that 'Lish was a little nobler than Threat, and they laid to vote according.

"If only the town could get rousted up somehow," Mis' Toplady kep' saying, grieving. "It seems as if, if there was something to roust folks, they'd do something. And if they'd only do something, they'd get rousted. It's like a snake with its tail in its mouth. It seems as if, if we could have some doin's on election day—oh, I wish't we was a real human being," she says, again and again, "I wish't we was. I bet we'd wind this town up, and we wouldn't set it by Threat's watch nor by 'Lish's, either. We'd set it by the sun."

But we see we couldn't take no part. And the town settled down on its oars restful, waiting for election day that looked like it wasn't going to do nothing but shake up the town feather-bed and lay it back on springs that sagged in the same old place.

Three days before election it happened I was up early to mix my bread. The clock showed half-past six just as I got through with my breakfast, and the sun come in so nice and slanting acrost my kitchen floor that I stepped to the open door to get the smell of it. All outside lay sweet and surprised, like the first notes of something being played. Before I knew it, I went out and down the path, between the things that hadn't come up yet—ain't it like all outdoors was friendly and elbow near, the way it keeps pulling at you to be out there with it? Before I knew it I was out my back gate and acrost the vacant lot and off down the old trail road, my hands wrapped up in my apron and me being just selfish glad I was alive.

With outdoors all around you, just waiting to be paid attention to; with friends set here and there in the world, near like planets, high and single like stars, or grouped like constellations; and with a spirit inside us—the same spirit—trying to say something—and trying to say the same thing—ain't life rich? Ain't it rich?

Sometimes I try to think what could make it richer. And I can never get any farther than the growing of those three foundation things: Outdoors and friends and the spirit. For life will be richer when the outdoors gets done—the floods tamed, the roads built, the forests tended, the deserts risen from the dead and the cities and towns and villages tamed and built and trained and tended and risen from the dead of dirt and ugliness to be real bodies for the souls stirring and beating in them now—and trying to speak. And life will be richer when friends come true—not just this planet, and that star, and these constellations,—but when the whole great company of friends, in homes, in churches, in mines, in prisons, in factories, in brothels, shall be known to us, and set free to be real bodies for the souls stirring and beating in them now—and trying to speak. And not till then will that spirit in outdoors and in cities and in us—the same spirit, trying to say the same thing—not till then can that spirit ever get it said.

"Oh," I thought, "on a morning like this, if somebody could only think of the right word, maybe the whole thing might come true."

And almost I knew what that word was—like you do.

I remember I wasn't thinking of anything but wonder, when away acrost the Pump pasture I see a thing. It wasn't a tent or it wasn't a wagon or it wasn't a farm machine of any kind. I looked at it a minute and I couldn't formulate nothing. And as you could drive through the Pump pasture fence 'most anywheres, I went through and started right over to whatever was there.

'Most anybody can tell you how it looked, for by nine o'clock the whole village was out to it. But I'll never be able to tell much about the feel of the minute when I see the two great silk wings and the airy wire, and knew I was coming close up to a flying-machine, setting there on the ground, like a god that had stopped on a knoll to tie his shoe.

A man was down on his hands and knees, doing something to an underneath part of it, but I guess at first I hardly see him. The machine was the thing, the machine that could go up in the air, the machine that *had done it at last*!

"Good morning," says the man, all of a sudden. "Am I trespassing?"

He stood there with his cap in his hand, clean-muscled, youngish, easy-acting, and as casual as if he'd just come out of a doorway instead of out of the sky.

I says, "Ain't it wonderful? Ain't it wonderful?" Which is just exactly what I'd said about Mis' Toplady's crocheted bed-spread. It's terrible to try to talk with nothing but the dictionary back of you.

"Yes," he says, "it is. Then I'm not trespassing?"

"No more'n the eagles of the Lord," I says to him. "Are you broke down?"

"There's a little something wrong with the balance," he says. "I'm going to lie over here a day or so, providing the eagle of the Lord figure holds for the town. What place will this be?" he asks.

"Friendship Village," I says.

"Friendship Village," he says it after me, and looked off at it. And I stood for a minute looking at it, too.

Beyond the trees north of the pasture it lay, with little lifts of smoke curling up from folks's cook-stoves. There was a look to it of breakfasts a-getting and stores being opened and the day rousting up. Right while we looked, the big, bass seven o'clock whistle blew over to the round-house, and the little peepy one chimed in up at the brick-yard, and I could hear the town clock in the engine-house striking, kind of old-fashioned and sweet-toned. And all around the country lay quiet-seeming, down to the flats and out across the tracks and clear to the city limits that we couldn't see, where the life of the little fields was going on. And in that nice, cozy, seven-o'clock minute I see it all as I do sometimes, almost like a person sitting there, with its face turned towards me, expectant, waiting to see what I'm going to do for it.

"Jove," says the man, "look at it! Look at it. It looks like the family sitting down to breakfast."

I glanced up at him quick. Not many sees villages that way. The most sees them like cats asleep in the sun. But I always like to think of 'em like a room—a little room in the house, full of its family, real busy getting the room-work done up in time.

"From here," I says, "it does most look like a real town."

"More folks live in the little towns of the United States than in the big cities of it," he said, absent.

"They *do*?" I says.

"By count," he answers, nodding, and stood a minute looking over at the roofs and the water tower. "You feel that," he says, "when you see them the way I do. From up high. I keep seeing them skimming under me, little places whose names don't show. And it always seems that way—like the family at breakfast—or working—or sitting around the arc lamp. You're splendid—you little towns. What you do is what the world does."

A kind of shiver took me in the back of my head.

"It looks as if such nice things were going on over there—in Friendship Village," he says, his voice sort of wrapping about the name.

"Election day is going on," I says, "day after to-morrow. But it won't be so very nice."

"No," he says, "they aren't very nice—yet."

That made me think of something. "Have you been in many cities and dropped down into many towns?" I ask' him.

"Several," says he,—sort of rueful.

"On election day?" I says.

"Sometimes," he answered.

"Well, then," I says, "maybe you can tell me what they do on election day in cities. Don't they ever have exercises?"

"Exercises?" he says over, blank.

"Why, yes," I says, "though I dunno just how I mean that. But don't they ever open up the city hall and have singing and speeches—not political speeches, but ones about folks and about living? I should think they must do that somewheres—'most anybody would of thought of that. And have the young folks there, and have them that's going to vote sort of—well, *commenced*, like college. Don't they do that, places?"

When he shook his head I was worried for fear he'd think I was crazy.

"No," he says, "I never heard of their doing that anywhere—yet."

But when he says that "yet" I wasn't worried any more. And I burst right out and told him about our trouble in Friendship Village, and about the "best" people never voting, and the city limits folks not coming in for it, and about our two candidates, and about Eppleby, that hadn't a ghost of a show.

"Us ladies," I wound up, "wanted to have a kind of an all-together campaign—with mass meetings of folks to kind of talk over the town, mutual. And we wanted to get up some exercises to make election day a real true day, and to roust folks up to being not so very far from the way things was meant to be. But the men folks said it wasn't never done so. They give us that reason."

The bird-man looked at me, and nodded. "I fancy it isn't," he says, "—yet."

But he didn't say anything else, and I thought he thought I was woman-foolish; so to cover up, I says, hasty:

"*Could* you leave me hear you talk a little about it? I mean about flying. It's old to you, but it's after-I-die to me. I never shall do it. So far I've never seen it. But oh, I like to hear about it. It seems the freest-feeling thing we've ever done."

"To do," he says, "it's coldish. And it's largely acrobatics—yet. But to see—yes, I fancy it is about the freest-feeling thing we've ever done. A thing," he says my words over, smiling a little, "that makes you think you're a step nearer to the way things were meant to be." Then he stood still a minute, looking down at me meditative. "Has there ever been a flying-machine in Friendship Village?" he ask' me.

"Never," I says—and my heart stood still at what it thought of.

"And day after to-morrow is your election day?" he says over.

"Yes," I says—and my head begun to beat like my heart wasn't.

"The machine will be in shape by then," he said. "Would—would you care to have me make a flight on election-day morning? Free, you know. It wouldn't be much; but it might," he says, with his little smile, "it might pull in a few votes from the edge of town."

"Oh, my land—oh, my land a-living!" I says—and couldn't say another word.

But I knew he knew what I meant. It was a dream like I hadn't ever dreamed of dreaming. It seems it was his own machine—he was on his own hook, a-pleasuring. And it seemed as if he just had come like an eagle of the Lord, same as I said.

We settled where I was to let him know, and then I headed for Mis' Toplady's, walking some on the ground and some in the air. For I sensed the thing, whole and clear, so be we could get enough to pitch in. And Mis' Toplady left her breakfast dishes setting, like I had mine, and away we went. And I see Mis' Toplady's ideas was occupying her whole face.

We went straight to the mothers—Mis' Uppers and Mis' Merriman and Mis' Sturgis and the others that had sons that was going to vote, this year or in ten years or in twenty years. I dunno whether it was the mother in them, or just the straight human being in them—but they see, the most of 'em, what it was we meant. Of course some of them just see the lark, and some of them just didn't want to refuse us, and some of them just joined in because they're the joining-in kind. But oh, some of them see what we see—and it was something shining and real and far off, and it made us willing to go ahead like wild, and I dunno but like mad. Ain't it wonderful how when a plan is born into the world, it grows on air? On air—and a little pitching in to work?

All but Mis' Silas Sykes. When we went to see her, Mis' Sykes was like that much adamant.

"Pshaw," says Mis' Sykes, "you ladies don't understand politics. In politics you can't fly up this way and imagine out vain things. You got to do 'em like they've been done. As I understand it, they's two parties. One is for the good of the country and one ain't. And anything you dicker up outside them two gets the public all upset and steps on the Constitution. And Silas says you've got to handle the Constitution like so many eggs, or else where does the United States come in?"

"It don't seem to me that all makes real good sense," says Mis' Toplady, troubled.

"No," says Mis' Sykes, serene, "the people as a whole never do see sense. It's always a few that has to do the seeing."

"I know," says Mis' Toplady, "I know. But what I think is this: *Which few?*"

"Why, them that best supports the party measures," says Mis' Sykes, superior.

But Mis' Toplady, she shook her head.

"It don't follow out," she says, firm. "Legs ain't the only things they is to a chair."

Nor, as us ladies saw it, the polls ain't all there is to election day. And we done what we could, steadfast and quick and together, up to the very night before the day that was the day.

On election-day morning, I woke up before daylight and tried to tell if the sun was going to shine. The sky wasn't up there yet—nothing was but the airful of dark. But acrost the street I see a light in a kitchen—it was at the station agent's that had come home to the hot breakfast his wife had been up getting for him. One of 'em come out to the well for a bucket of water, and the pulleys squeaked, and somebody's dog woke up and barked. Back on the trail road somebody's baby was crying. Down acrost the draw the way-freight whistled and come rumbling in. And there was Friendship Village, laying still, being a town in the dark with nobody looking, just like it was being one all day long, with people looking on but never sensing what they saw.

It seemed, though, as if they must get it through their heads that day that the town was being a town right before their face and eyes—having a kind of a performance to do, like digestion, or thinking, or working; and having something anxious and fluttered inside of it, waiting to know what was going to become of it. I could almost sense this at six o'clock, when Mis' Toplady and I hurried down to the market square. Yes, sir, six o'clock in the morning it was. We had engineered it that the flight of the flying-machine should be at seven o'clock, so's everybody could have a chance to see it on their way to work, and so's they should be at the market-square doings before they went to the polls.

The sun *was* shining like mad, and the place looked all expectant and with that ready-to-nod look that anything got ready beforehand will always put on. Only this seemed sort of a special nod. We'd had a few board seats put up, and a platform that 'most everybody had the idea the airship was going up from. The machine itself was over in the corner of the square near the wood-yard under a wagon-shed they'd made over for it. And to a stand near the platform the Friendship Married Ladies' Cemetery Improvement Sodality had advertised to serve hot coffee and hot griddle-cakes and sausages. And we begun on the coffee and the sausages long enough ahead so's by the time folks was in the high midst of arriving, the place smelled like a kitchen with savory things a-doing on the cook-stove.

And I tell you, folks done some arriving. Us ladies had seen to it to have the flight advertised big them two nights. The paper done it willing enough, being the bird-man was so generous and all. Then everybody's little boy had been posted off as far as the city limits with hand-bills and posters, advertising the flight, and the breakfast on election day. And it seemed to me that outside the place we'd roped off, and in wagons in the streets, was 'most everybody in Friendship Village that I ever knew or saw. The folks from the little city-limit farms, the folks that ordinarily didn't have time to vote nor to take a holiday, even folks from the country and from other towns, "best" people and all—they was all there to see the sky-wagon.

The bird-man had to dicker away quite a little at his machine. A man had run out from the city to help him, and out there with them was Lem Toplady and Jimmy Sturgis and Hugh Merriman, and two-three more of those boys, that had got acquainted with the bird-man. And while they was getting ready, the band was playing gay over in the bandstand, and we was serving breakfasts as fast as we could hand them out. Mis' Sturgis was doing the coffee, I was sizzling sausages that the smell floated up and down Daphne Street delicious, and Mis' Toplady was frying the pancakes because she's had such a big family to fry for she's lightning in the right wrist.

Everybody was talking and laughing and waiting their turn, and acting as if they liked it. Them that was up around the breakfast stand didn't seem to be saying much about politics. Us ladies mentioned to one another that Threat nor 'Lish didn't seem to be anywhere around. But we was mostly all thinking just about the flying-machine, and how nice it was to be having it, and about the socialness of it all—like the family was having breakfast....

Just as the big, bass seven-o'clock whistle trailed out from the round-house—the brick-yard one didn't blow because the men was all at the market square—the thing happened that we'd arranged for. Down Daphne Street, hurrying some because they was late, with irregular marching and a good deal of laughing, come the public-school teachers with the school children. We'd give out that they'd be easier managed so, and not so much under foot; but what we really wanted was that they should come in just like this, together, and set together, because we wanted something of them after a while.

They sat down on the place we'd left for 'em, on the seats and the grass in front of everybody, and them that could sing we put on the platform, lots of rows deep, so's they all covered it. They was big boys and little, and little girls and big, good-dressed and poor-dressed; with honest fathers, and with them that didn't know honest when they see it nor miss it when they didn't—and all of them was the Friendship Village that's going to be some time, when the market square is emptied of us others, for good and all.

"Where's Threat and 'Lish?" I says to Eppleby, that was helping keep the children in order.

"Dustin' the mayor's office out ready, I s'pose," he says, wrinkling his eyes at the corners.

"Mebbe they've abducted each other," Mis' Toplady suggests, soothing.

Mis' Sykes looked over from filling the syrup pitchers—she'd boiled the brown sugar down for that, and it added its thick, golden smell unto the general inviting mixture.

"I don't think," she says serious, "that you'd ought to speak disrespectful of *any*body that's going to be your mayor. Public officials," said she, "had ought to be paid respect to, or else the law won't be carried out."

"Shucks," says Mis' Toplady, short. She'd made upwards of ninety griddle cakes by then, and she was getting kind of flustered and crispy.

"Shucks?" says Mis' Sykes, haughty and questioning, and all but in two syllables.

"If that's all the law is," says Mis' Toplady, beating away at her pancake batter, "give me anar-kicky, or whatever it is they call it."

Mis' Sykes never said a word. She just went on making syrup, reproachful. Mis' Sykes is one of them that acts like life was made up of the pattern of things, and like speaking of warf and woof wasn't delicate. And she never so much as lets on they is such a thing as a knot. Yes, some folks is like that. But not me—not me.

It was 'most half-past seven o'clock when the bird-man was ready. Like a big bug the machine looked, with spidery, bent legs and wings spread ready and no head necessary. And when he finally run it off down the square and headed towards the Pump pasture, my heart sunk some. My land, I thought, it can't be a real true one. I guess there are them, but this right here on the market square can't be one.

Since the world begun, there ain't a more wonderful minute for folks than the minute when they first see some kind of flying-machine leave the ground—*leave the ground!* It's like seeing the future come true right in your face. The thing done it so gentle and so simple that you'd of thought it was invented when legs was. It lifted itself up in the air, like by its own bootstraps, and it went up and up and up, just like going up was its own alphabet. It went and it kept going, its motor buzzing and purring, softer and softer. And pretty soon the blue that it was going up to meet seemed to come down and meet it, and the two sort of joined, and the big, wide gold morning flowed all over them, and the first thing I knew the bird-man's machine and him in it looked like just what I had said: an eagle of the Lord, soaring to meet the sun like a friend of its.

I couldn't bear it any more. It seemed to me as if, if I should look any longer, I should all of a sudden have ten senses instead of five, and they'd explode me. I looked away and down. And when I done that, all at once there I was looking right into the face of all the folks in Friendship Village. Heads back, a sea of little white dabs that was faces, and hearts beating underneath where you couldn't see 'em—all of us was standing there breathless, feeling just alike. Feeling just alike and being just alike, underneath that wonderful thing happening in the sky.... And all of a sudden, while I looked at them, the faces all blurred and wiggled, and it seemed like I was looking into only one face, the face of Friendship Village, like a person....

I see it, like I'd never seen it before. While we watched, *we was one person.* When we was all thinking about the same thing, there was only one of us. And the more wonderful things that come into the world and took hold of everybody, the more *one* we was going to get and to stay. And this, all vague inside of us, I knew now was what us ladies had meant by what we'd planned. Didn't it seem—didn't it seem as if them that watched had ought to stay *one*—that decent, wondering, almost reverent one, long enough to vote decent and wondering and reverent for their town?

Right while my heart was beating with it all, the little buzzing and purring of the motor, away up there in the blue, stopped short off. My eyes flew up again, and I see the bird-man coming down. He was up so high that he was a dot, and he grew and grew like a thing being born in the sky—right down towards us and on us he come like a shot, a shot-down shot. Nobody breathed. I couldn't see. But I looked and looked and dreaded.... And not eight hundred feet from the ground he begun coming down easy, and he come the rest of the way as gentle as a bird, and lit where he rose from.

Oh, how they cheered him—like one man! *Like one man.* Lem Toplady and Jimmy Sturgis, Jr., and the boys that was out in the field went and shook his hand—like the servants, I thought in the middle of my head, of some great new order. And I was thinking so deep and so breathless that I 'most forgot the band till it crashed right out behind us, playing loud and fine that Marseilles French piece, like we'd told them. And when it done that, up hopped the children that it give the cue to, and there in the midst of us they struck in, singing loud and clear the words they sung in school to that old tune, with its wonderful tang to it, that slips to your heels with its music and makes you want to go start something and to start it *them*:

"Come, Children of To-morrow, come!
New glory dawns upon the world.
The ancient banners must be furled.
The earth becomes our common home—
The earth becomes our common home.
From plain and field and town there sound
The stirring rumors of the day.
Old wrongs and burdens must make way
For men to tread the common ground.

"Look up! The children win to their immortal place.
March on, march on—within the ranks of all the human race.

"Come, love of people, for the part
Invest our willing arms with might.
Mother of Liberty, shed light
As on the land, so in the heart—
As on the land, so in the heart.
Divided, we have long withstood
The love that is our common speech.
The comrade cry of each to each
Is calling us to humanhood."

Hum it to the tune of that Marseilles piece, and you'll know how we was all feeling. By the time they got down to their last two lines, my throat was about the size of my head.

And then the bird-man got back in his little sulky seat, and he waved his hand to us, and he left his machine run down the field, and lift, and head straight for open country. His way lay, it seemed, right acrost Friendship Village; and he'd no more'n started before the band started too, playing the tune that by now was in everybody's veins. And behind them the children fell in, singing again, and with the people streaming behind them they all marched off down Daphne Street—where the little shops lay waiting to be opened, and the polls was waiting to be voted in, and Friendship Village was waiting for us to know it was a town, like it meant.

All us ladies went to scraping up plates like fury. Excep' Mis' Toplady. She stood for a minute wiping her eyes on a paper napkin. And she says:

"Oh, ladies. I ain't never felt so much like a human being since I was born one."

And me, I stood there looking across the Market Square to the school-house. There it was, with its doors open and the new voting machine setting in the hall,—they'd took the polls out of the barber shop and the livery stable sole because the voting machine got in the way of trade. They'd put it in the school-house. And it was to the school-house that the men were going now.

"Oh," I says to Mis' Toplady, "would you think anybody could go in a child's school-house, and vote for anybody that—"

"No, no," she says, "you wouldn't think so, would you?"

But she didn't look at me. She was looking over to the school-house steps. Lem Toplady stood there, and Jimmy Sturgis, Jr., and Hugh Merriman and Mis' Uppers's boy—watching the last of the bird-man and the air-wagon flying down the sky. When it had gone, the four boys turned and went together up the steps of the school-house. And Mis' Toplady and Mis' Sturgis and Mis' Fire Chief Merriman and Mis' Uppers stood and watched them—going in to vote now, to the place where the four mothers had seen them go ever since they were little bits of boys, with faces and clothes to be kept clean, and lessons to learn, and lunch baskets to fill. Then the mothers could either do these things for them—or anyway help along. Now they stood there doing nothing, watching, while their boys went in to do their first vote—into the school-house where they'd learned their A B C's.

"Ain't that—ain't it just—?" I says low to Mis' Toplady; and kind of stopped.

"Ain't it?" she says, fervent and low too. "Oh, ain't it?"

"The time'll come," I says, "when you mothers, and me too, will go in there with them. And when we'll go straight from a great public meeting—like this—to a great public business like that. And when it comes—"

We all looked at one another—all but Mis' Silas Sykes, that was busy with the syrup pitchers. But the thing was over the rest of us—the lift and the courage and the belief of that hour we'd all had together. And I says out:

"Oh, ladies! I believe in us. I believe in us."

So I tell you, I wasn't surprised at what that day done. I dunno for sure what done it. Mebbe it was just the common sense in folks that I can*not* get over believing in. Mebbe it was the cores of their minds that I know is sound, no matter how many soft spots disfigures their brains. Mebbe it was the big power and the big glory that's near us, waiting to be drawn-on-and-used as fast as we learn how to do it—no, I dunno for sure.

But they put Eppleby Holcomb in for mayor. Eppleby got in, to mayor the town! And some said it was because the boys that was to cast their first vote had got out, last minute, and done some hustling, unbeknownst. And some thought it was because Threat and 'Lish couldn't wait, but done a little private celebrating together in Threat's hotel bar the night before election. And others said election always is some ticklish—they give that reason.

But me—I went and stood out on my side porch that election-day night, a-looking down Daphne Street to the village. There it lay, with its arc light shining blue by the Market Square, and it was being a village, with nobody looking and all its folks in its houses, just like the family around that one evening lamp. And their hearts was beating along about the same things; just like they had beat that day for the sky-wagon, and for the Marseilles French piece. Only they didn't know it—yet.

And I says right out loud to the village—just like Friendship Village was a person, with its face turned toward me, listening:

"Why, you ain't half of us—nor you ain't some of us. You're all of us! And you must of known it all the time."

THE FLOOD

It's "brother" now and it's "brother" then,
And it's "brother" another day,
And it's "brother" whenever a loud doom sounds
With a terrible toll to pay....
But what of the silent dooms they bear
In an inoffensive way?

It's "brother" here and it's "brother" there,
And it's "brother" once in a while,
And it's "brother" whenever an hour hangs black
On the face of the common dial....
But what of the days that stretch between
For the march of the rank and file?

    I don't know how well you know villages, but I hope you know anyhow one, because if you don't they's things to life that you don't know yet. Nice things.

    I was thinking of that the Monday morning that all Friendship Village remembers still. I was walking down Daphne Street pretty early, seeing everybody's breakfast fire smoke coming out of the kitchen chimney and hearing everybody's little boy splitting wood and whistling out in the chip pile, and smelling everybody's fried mush and warmed-up potatoes and griddle cakes come floating out sort of homely and old fashioned and comfortable, from the kitchen cook-stoves.

    "Look at the Family," I says to myself, "sitting down to breakfast, all up and down the street."

    And when the engine-house clock struck seven, and the whistle over to the brick-yard blew little and peepy and like it wasn't sure it was seven but it thought so, and the big whistle up to the round-house blew strong and hoarse and like it knew it all and could tell you more about the time of day then you'd ever guessed if it wanted to, and the sun come shining down like the pouring out of some new thing that we'd never had before—I couldn't help drawing a long breath, just because Now was Now.

    Down the walk a little ways I met Bitty Marshall. I wondered a little at seeing him on the street way up our end o' town. He'd lately opened a little grocery store down on the Flats, for the Folks that lived down there. Him and his wife lived overhead, with a lace curtain to one of the front windows—though they was two front windows to the room. "I've always hankered for a pair o' lace curtains," she said to me when I went up to see her one day, "but when I'd get the money together to buy 'em, it seems like somethin' has always come and et it up—medicine or school books or the children's shoes. So when we moved in here, I says I was goin' to have one lace curtain to one window if I board the other up!" And she had one to one window, and a green paper shade to the other.

"Well, Bitty," I says, "who's keeping store to-day? Your wife?"

But he didn't smile gay, like he usually does. He looked just regular.

"Neither of us'll be doing it very long," he said. "I've got to close down."

"But I thought it was paying you nice?" I says.

"And so it was," says Bitty, "till Silas Sykes took a hand. He didn't have a mind to see me run no store down there and take away his trade from the Flats. He begun under-sellin' me—he's been runnin' everything off at cost till I can't hold out no longer."

"So that's what Silas Sykes has been slashin' down everything for, from prunes upwards," I says. "I might of known. I might of known."

"My interest is comin' due," says Bitty, movin' on; "I've come up this mornin' to see about going back to work in the brick-yard."

"Good land," I says sorrowful. "Good land. And Silas in the Council—and on the School Board—and an elder thrown in."

Bitty grinned a little then.

"It ain't new," he says, over his shoulder. And he went on up the street, holding his hands heavy, and kind of letting his feet fall instead of setting them down, like men walk that don't care, any more.

I understood what he meant when he said it wasn't new. There was Joe Betts that worked three years getting his strawberry bed going, and when he begun selling from the wagon instead of taking to Silas Sykes at the Post-Office store, Silas got the Council that he's in to put up licenses, clear over Joe's head. And Ben Dole, he'd got a little machine and begun making cement blocks for folks's barns, and Timothy Toplady, that's interested in the cement works over to Red Barns, got Zachariah Roper, that's to the head of the Red Barns plant, to come over and buy Ben Dole's house and come up on his rent—two different times he done that. It wasn't new. But it all kind of baffled me. It seemed so legal that I couldn't put down my finger on what was the matter. Of course when a thing's legal, and you're anyways patriotic, you are some put to it to find a real good term to blame it with. I walked along, thinking about it, and feeling all baffled up as to what to do. But I hadn't gone ten steps when I thought of one thing I could do, to clear up my own i-dees if for nothing else. I turned around and called out after Bitty.

"Oh, Bitty," I says, "would you mind me letting Silas know I know?"

He threw out his hands a little, and let 'em kind of set down side of him.

"Why sure not," he said, "but if you're thinkin' of saying anything to him—best spare the breath."

"We'll see about that," I thought, and I went on down Daphne Street with a Determination sitting up in the air just ahead of me, beginning to crook its finger at me to come along.

In a minute I come past Mis' Fire Chief Merriman's house. The Chief has been dead several years, but we always keep calling her by his title, same as we call the vacant lot by the depot the Ellsworth House, though the Ellsworth House has been burned six years and it's real kind of confusing to strangers that we try to direct. I remember one traveling man that headed right out towards the marsh and missed his train because some of us had told him to keep straight on till he turned the corner by the Ellsworth House, and he kept hunting for it and trusting in it till he struck the swamp. But you know how it is—you get to saying one thing, and you keep on uttering it after the thing is dead and gone and another has come in its place, and when somebody takes you up on it, like as not you'll tell him he ain't patriotic. It was the same with the Fire Chief. Dead though he was, we always give her his official title, because we'd got headed calling her that and hated to stop. She was out in her garden that morning, and I stood still when I caught sight of her tulips. They looked like the earth had broke open and let out a leak of what's inside it, never intending to show so much at once.

"Mis' Merriman," I says, "what tulips! Or," says I, flattering, "is it a bon-fire, with lumps in the flame?"

Mis' Merriman was bending over, setting out her peony bulbs, with her back to me. When I first spoke, she looked over her shoulder, and then she went right on setting them out, hard as she could dig. "Glad you like *something* that belongs to me," says she, her words kind of punched out in places by the way she dug.

Then I remembered. Land, I'd forgot all about it. But at the last meeting of the Friendship Married Ladies' Cemetery Improvement Sodality—we don't work for just Cemetery any more, but we got started calling it that twenty years back, and on we go under that name, serene as a straight line—at that last meeting I'd appointed Mis' Timothy Toplady a committee of one to go to the engine-house to get them to leave us sell garbage pails at cost in the front part; and it seems Mis' Merriman had give out that she'd ought to be the one to do it, along of her husband having been Fire Chief for eleven years and more, and she might have influence with 'em. I'd of known that too, if I'd thought of it—but you know how it is when they pitch on to you to appoint a committee from the chair? All your i-dees and your tact and your memory and your sense takes hold of hands and exits out of you, and you're left up there on the platform, unoccupied by any of 'em—and ten to one you'll appoint the woman with the thing in her hat that first attracts your attention. Mebbe it ain't that way with some, but I've noticed how it is with me, and that day I'd appointed Mis' Toplady to that committee sole because she passed her cough-drops just at that second and my eye was drawed acrost to them and to her. I'd never meant to slight Mis' Fire Chief and I felt nothing on this earth but kindness to her, and yet when I heard her speak so, all crispy and chilly and uppish, about being glad I liked *something* about her, all to once my veins sort of run starch, and my bones lay along in me like they was meant for extra pokers, and I flashed out back at her:

"Oh, yes, Mis' Merriman—your *tulips* is all right——" bringing my full heft down on the word "tulips."

And then I went on up the street with something—something—something inside me, or outside me, or mebbe just *with* me, looking at me, simple and grave and direct and patient and—wounded again. And I felt kind of sick, along up and down my chest. And the back of my head begun to hurt. And I breathed fast and without no pleasure in taking air. And I says to myself and the world and the Something Else:

"Oh, God, creator of heaven and earth that's still creatin' 'em as fast as we'll get our meannesses out of the way and let you go on—*what* made me do that?"

And nothing told me what—not then.

Just then I see Mis' Holcomb-that-was-Mame Bliss come out on their side porch and hang out the canary. I waved my hand acrost to her, and she whips off her big apron and shakes it at me, and I see she was feeling the sun shine clear through her, just like I'd been.

"Come on down with me while I do an errant," I calls to her.

"My table ain't cleared off yet," says she, decisive.

"Mine either," I says back. "But ain't you just as fond of the sun in heaven as you are of your own breakfast dishes? Come on."

So she took off her apron and run in and put on a breastpin and come down the walk, rolling down her sleeves, and dabbing at her hair to make sure, and we went down the street together. And the first thing I done was to burst out with my thoughts all over her, and I told her about Silas and about Bitty Marshall, and about how his little store on the Flats was going to shut down.

"Well," she says, "if that ain't Silas all over. If it ain't Silas. I could understand his dried fruit sales, 'long toward Spring so—it's easy to be reasonable about dried peaches when its most strawberry time. I could even understand his sales on canned stuff he's had in the store till the labels is all fly-specked. But when he begun to cut on new potatoes and bananas and Bermuda onions and them necessities, I says to myself that he was goin' to get it back from somewheres. So it's out o' Bitty Marshall's pocket, is it?"

"And it's so legal, Mis' Holcomb," I says, "it's so bitterly legal. Silas ain't corporationed himself in with nobody. It ain't as if the courts could get after him and some more and make them be fair to their little competitors, same as courts is fallin' over themselves to get the chance to do. This is nothin' but Silas—our leadin' citizen."

Mis' Holcomb, she made her lips both thin and tight.

"Let's us go see Silas," says she, and I see my Determination was crooking its finger to her, same as to me.

Silas had gone down to the store, we found, but Mis' Sykes was just coming out their gate with a plate of hot Johnny cake to take up to Miss Merriman.

"Oh, Mis' Sykes," I says, "is your night bloomin' cereus goin' to be out to-night, do you know? I heard it was." The whole town always watches for Mis' Sykes's night-blooming cereus to bloom, and the night it comes out we always drop in and set till quite late.

Mis' Sykes never looked at Mis' Holcomb.

"Good morning, Calliope," says she. "Yes, I think it will, Calliope. Won't you come in to-night, Calliope, and see it?" says she.

I says I would; and when we went on,

"What struck her," I says, puzzled, "to spread my name on to what she said like that, I wonder? I feel like I'd been planted in that sentence of hers in three hills."

Then I see Mis' Holcomb's eyes was full of tears.

"Mis' Sykes was trying to slight me," she says. "She done that so's to kind of try to seem to leave me out."

"Well," I says, "I must say, she sort of succeeded. But what for?"

"I give her potato bread receipt away," she says miserable, "and it seems she didn't expect it of me."

"Is *that* it?" I says. "Well, of course we both know Mis' Sykes ain't the one to ever forgive a thing like that. I s'pose she'll socially ostrich-egg you—or whatever it is they say?"

"I s'pose she will," says Mis' Holcomb forlorn. "You know how Mis' Sykes is. From now on, if I say the sky is blue, Mis' Sykes'll say no, pink."

They was often them feuds in Friendship Village—like this one, and like Mis' Merriman's and my new one. It hadn't ought to be so in a village family, but then sometimes it is. I s'pose in cities it's different—they always say it makes folks broader to live in cities, and they prob'ly get to know better. But it's like that with us.

Well, of course the back-bone had dropped out of the morning for Mis' Holcomb, and she didn't take no more interest in going down street than she would in darning—I mention darning because I defy anybody to pick out anything uninterestinger. Up to the time I got to the Post-Office Hall store, I was trying to persuade her to come in with me to see Silas.

"I'd best not go in," she says. "You know how one person's quarrel is catching in a family. And a potato bread receipt is as good as anything else to be loyal about."

But I made her go in, even if she shouldn't say a word, but just act constituent-like.

Silas was alone in the store, sticking dates on to a green paste-board to make the word "Pure" to go over his confectionery counter. He had his coat off, and his hair had been brushed with a wet brush that left the print of the bristles, and his very back looked Busy.

"Hello, folks," says he, "how's life?"

"Selfish as ever," I says. "Ain't trade?"

"Well," says Silas, "it's every man for himself and the devil take the hindmost in most everything now, ain't it? As the prophet said, It beats all."

"It does that," I says. "It beats everybody in the end. Funny they don't find it out. That's why," I adds serene, "we been so moved by your generous cost sales of stuff, Silas. What you been doin' that for anyway?" I put it to him.

"For to bait trade," says he.

"For what else?" I ask' him.

"Why," he says, beginning to be irritable, which some folks uses instead of wit, "to push the store, of course. I ain't been doin' it for the fun of it."

"Ain't you now?" I says. "I thought it was kind of a game with you."

"What do you mean—game?" says Silas, scowling.

"Cat and mouse," I says brief. "You the cat and Bitty Marshall the mouse."

Silas stood up straight and just towered at me.

"What you been hearing *now*?" he says, demandful.

"Well," I answered him, "nothing that surprised me very much. Only that you've been underselling Bitty so's to drive him out and keep the trade of the Flats yourself."

Silas never squinched.

"Well," says he, "what if I have? Ain't I got a right to protect my own business?"

I looked him square in the eye.

"No," I says, "not that way."

Silas put back his head and laughed, tolerant.

"I guess," he says, "you ain't been following very close the business affairs of this country."

"Following them was how I come to understand about you," I says simple. And I might have added, "And knowing about you, I can see how it is with them."

For all of a sudden, I see how he thought of these things, and for a minute it et up my breath. It had always seemed to me that men that done things like this to other folks's little business was wicked men *in general*. That they kind of got behind being legal and grinned out at folks and said: "Do your worst. You can't stop us." But now I see, like a blast of light, that it was no such thing; but that most of them was probably good husbands and fathers, like Silas; industrious, frugal, members of the Common Councils and of the school boards, elders in the church, charitable, kindly, and believing simple as the day that what they was doing was for the good of business. Business.

"Well," Silas was saying, "what you going to do about it?"

I looked back at Marne Holcomb standing, nervous, over by the cranberry barrel:

"I've got this to do about it," I says, "and I know Mame Holcomb has, and between us we can get every woman in Friendship Village to do the same—unless it is your wife that can't help herself like lots of women can't: Unless you get your foot off Bitty's neck, every last one of us will quit buying of you and go down to the Flats and trade with Bitty. How about it, Mame?"

She spoke up, like them little women do sometimes that you ain't ever looked upon as particularly special when it comes to taking a stand.

"Why, yes," she says. "They ain't a woman in the village that would stand that kind of dealing, if they only knew. And we," she adds tranquil, "could see to that."

Silas give the date-word he was making a throw over on to the sugar barrel, and made a wild gesture with a handful of toothpicks.

"Women," he says, "dum women. If it wasn't for you women swarming over the world like different kinds of—of—of—noxious insects, it would be a regular paradise."

"Sure it would," I says logical, "because there wouldn't be a man in it to mess it up."

Silas had just opened his mouth to reply, when all of a sudden, like a letter in your box, somebody come and stood in the doorway—a man, and called out something, short and sharp and ending in "Come on—all of you," and disappeared out again, and we heard him running down the street. Then we saw two-three more go running by the door, and we heard some shouting. And Silas, that must have guessed at what they said, he started off behind them, dragging on his sear-sucker coat and holding his soft felt hat in his mouth, it not seeming to occur to him that he could set it on his head till he was ready to use it.

"What's the matter?" I says to Mis' Holcomb. "They must be getting excited because nothing ever happens here. They ain't nothing else to get excited over that I can think of."

Then we see more men come running, and their boots clumped down on the loose board walk with that special clump and thud that boots gets to 'em when they're running with bad news, or hurrying for help.

"What is it?" I says, getting to the door. And I see men begin to come out of the stores and get in knots and groups that you can tell mean trouble of some kind, just as plain as you can tell that some portraits of total strangers is the portraits of somebody that's dead. They look dead. And them groups looked trouble. And then I see Timothy Toplady come tearing down the road in his spring wagon, with his horse's check reins all dragging and him lashing out at 'em as he stood up in the box. Then I run right out in the road and yelled at him.

"Timothy," I says, "what's the matter? What's happened?"

He drew up his horses, and threw out his hand, beckoning angular.

"Come on!" he says, "get in here—get in quick...."

Then he looked back over his shoulder and see Mis' Merriman that had come out to her gate with Mis' Sykes, and they was both out on the street, looking, and he beckoned, wild, to them; and they come running.

"Quick!" says Timothy. "The dam's broke. They've just telephoned everybody. The Flats'll be flooded. Come on and help them women load their things...."

I don't remember any of us saying a thing. We just clomb in over the back-board of Timothy's wagon, him reaching down to help us, courteous, and we set down on the bottom of the wagon—Mis' Holcomb and Mis' Sykes, them two enemies, and Mis' Merriman and me—and we headed for the Flats.

I remember, on the ride down there, seeing the street get thick with folks—in a minute the street was black with everybody, all hurrying toward what was the matter, and all veering out and swarming into the road—somehow, folks always flows over into the road when anything happens. And men and women kept coming out of houses, and calling to know what was the matter, and everybody shouted it back at them so's they couldn't understand, but they come out and joined in and run anyway. And over and over, as he drove, Timothy kept shouting to us how he had just been hitching up when the news come, and how his wagon was a new one and had ought to be able to cart off five or six loads at a trip.

"It can't hurt Friendship Village proper," I remember his saying over and over too, "that's built high and dry. But the whole Flats'll be flooded out of any resemblance to what they've been before."

"Friendship Village proper," I says over to myself, when we got to the top of Elephant Hill that let us look over the Pump pasture and away across the Flats, laying idle and not really counted in the town till it come to the tax list. There was dozens of little houses—the Marshalls and the Betts's and the Rickers's and the Hennings and the Doles and the Haskitts, and I donno who all. All our washings was done down there—or at least the washings was of them that didn't do them themselves. The garden truck of them that didn't have gardens, the home grown vegetables for Silas's store, the hired girls' homes of them that had hired girls, the rag man, the scissors grinder, Lowry that canes chairs and was always trying to sell us tomato plants—you know how that part of a town is populationed? And then there was a few that worked in Silas's factory, and an outlaying milkman or two—and so on. "Friendship Village proper," I says over and looked down and wondered why the Flats was improper enough to be classed in—laying down there in the morning sun, with nice, neat little door-yards and nice, neat little wreaths of smoke coming up out of their chimneys—and the whole Mad river loose and just going to swirl down on it and lap it up, exactly as hungry for it as if it had been Friendship Village "proper."

They was running out of their little houses, up towards us, coming with whatever they had, with children, with baskets between 'em, with little animals, with bed-quilts tied and filled with stuff. Some few we see was busy loading their things up on to the second floor, but most of 'em didn't have any second floors, so they was either running up the hill or getting a few things on to the roof. It wasn't a big river—we none of us or of them was afraid of any loss of life or of houses being tipped over or like that. But we knew there'd be two-three feet of water over their ground floors by noon.

"Land, land," says Mis' Sykes, that's our best housekeeper, "and I 'spose it's so late lots of 'em had their Spring cleaning done."

"I was thinkin' of that," says Mis' Holcomb, her enemy.

"But then it being so late most of 'em has got their winter vegetables et out of their sullars," says Mis' Merriman, trying to hunt out the bright side.

"That's true as fate, Mis' Merriman," I remember I says, agreeing with her fervent.

And us two pairs of feuds talked about it, together, till we got down into the Flats and begun helping 'em load.

We filled up the wagon with what they had ready, tied up and boxed up and in baskets or thrown in loose, and Timothy started back with the first load, Mis' Haskitt calling after him pitiful to be careful not to stomp on her best black dress that she'd started off with in her arms, and then trusted to the wagon and gone back to get some more. Timothy was going to take 'em up to the top of Elephant Hill and dump 'em there by appointment, and come back for another load, everybody sorting their own out of the pile later, as best they could. While he was gone we done things up for folks like wild and I donno but like mad, and had a regular mountain of 'em out on the walk when he come driving back; but when we got that all loaded on, out come Mis' Ben Dole, running with a whole clothes bars full of new-ironed clothes and begged Timothy to set 'em right up on top of the load, just as they was, and representing as they did Two Dollars' worth of washing and ironing for her, besides the value of the clothes that mustn't be lost. And Timothy took 'em on for her, and drove off balancing 'em with one hand, and all the clothes blowing gentle in the breeze.

I looked over to Mis' Holcomb, all frantic as she was, and it was so she looked at me.

"That was Ben Dole's wife that Timothy done that for," I says, to be sure we meant the same thing. "Just as if he hadn't never harmed her husband's cement plant."

"I know," says Mis' Holcomb. "Don't that beat the very day to a froth?" and she went on emptying Mis' Dole's bureau drawers into a bed-spread.

By the time the fourth load or so had gone on, and the other wagons that had come was working the same way, the water was seeping along the Lower Road, down past the wood-yard. More than one was saying we'd ought to begin to make tracks for high ground, because likely when it come, it'd come with a rush. And some of us had stepped out on the street and was asking Silas, that you kind of turn to in emergency, because he's the only one that don't turn to anybody else, whether we hadn't better go, when down the street we see a man come tearing like mad.

"My land," I says, "it's Bitty Marshall. He wasn't home. And where's his wife? I ain't laid eyes on her."

None of us had seen her that morning. And us that stood together broke into a run, and it was Silas and Mis' Merriman and me that run together, and rushed together up the stairs of Bitty's little grocery, to where he lived, and into the back room. And there set Bessie Marshall in the back room, putting her baby to sleep as tranquil as the blue sky and not knowing a word of what was going on, and by the window was Bitty's old mother, shelling pop-corn.

I never see anybody work like Silas worked them next few minutes. If he'd been a horse and a giant made one he couldn't have got more quick, necessary things out of the way. And we done what we could, and it wasn't any time at all till we was going down the stairs carrying what few things they'd most need for the next few days. When we stepped out in the street, the water was an inch or more all over where we stood, and when we'd got six steps from the house and Bitty had gone ahead shouting to the wagon, Bessie Marshall looked up at Silas real pitiful.

"Oh, Mr. Sykes," she says, "there's a coop of little chickens and their mother by the back door. Couldn't we take 'em?"

"Sure," says Silas, and when the wagon come he made it wait for us, and when the Marshalls and the baby and Mis' Merriman was seated in it, and me, he come running with the coopful of little yellow scraps, and we was the last wagon to leave the Flats and to get up to Elephant Hill again.

"But, oh," says Mis' Merriman grieving, "it seems like us women could do such a little bit of the rescuing. Oh, when it's a flood or a fire or a runaway, I do most question Providence as to why we wasn't all born men."

You know how it is, when a great big thing comes catastrophing down on you, it just eats up the edges of the thing you think with, and leaves you with nothing but the wish-bone of your brain operating, kind of flabby. But when we got up on top of Elephant Hill, where was everybody—folks from the Flats, and a good deal of what they owned put into a pile, and the folks from Friendship "proper" come to watch—there was Mis' Timothy Toplady already planning what to do, short off. Mis' Toplady can always connect up what's in her head with what's outside of it and—what's rarer still—with what's lacking outside of it.

"These folks has got to be fed," she says, "for the days of the high water. Bed and breakfast of course we can manage among us, but the other two meals is going to be some of a trick. So be Silas would leave us have Post Office hall free, we could order the stuff sent in right there, and all turn in and cook it."

"Oh, my," says Mis' Holcomb, soft, to me, "he'll never do that. He'll say it'll set a precedent, and what he does for one he'll have to do for all. It's a real handy dodge."

"Well," says Mis' Merriman, "leave him set a precedent for himself for floods. We won't expect it off him other."

"I ain't never yet seen him," I says, "carrying a chicken coop without he meant to sell chickens. Mebbe's he's got a change of heart. Let's ask him," I says, and I adds low to Mis' Toplady that I'd asked Silas for so many things that he wouldn't give or do that I could almost do it automatic, and I'd just as lives ask him again as not.

It wasn't but a minute till him and Timothy come by, each estimating how fast the river would raise. And I spoke up right then.

"Silas," I says, "had you thought how we're going to feed these folks till the water goes down?"

I fully expected him to snarl out something like he usually does, about us women being frantic to assume responsibility. Instead of that he looked down at us thoughtful:

"Well," says he, "that's just what I've been studying on some. And I was thinking that if you women would cook the stuff, us men would chip in and buy the material. And wouldn't it be some easier to cook it all in one place? I could let you have the Post Office hall, if you say so."

"Why, Silas," I says, "Silas ..." And I couldn't say another word. And it was the rest of 'em let him know that we'd do it. And when they'd gone on,

"Do you think Timothy sensed that?" says Mis' Toplady, meditative.

"I donno," says I, "but I can see to it that he does."

"I was only thinking," says she, "that we've got seven dozen fresh eggs in the house, and we're getting six quarts of milk a day now...."

"I'll recall 'em," says I, "to his mind."

But when I'd run ahead and caught up with 'em, and mentioned eggs and milk suggestive, in them quantities,

"Sure," says Timothy, "I just been telling Silas he could count on 'em."

And that was a wonderful thing, for we one and all knew Timothy Toplady as one of them decanter men that the glass stopper can't hardly be got out. But it wasn't the most wonderful—for Silas spoke up fervent—ferventer than I'd ever known him to speak:

"They can have anything we've got, Calliope," he says, "in our stores or our homes. Make 'em know that," says he.

It didn't take me one secunt to pull Silas aside.

"Silas," I says, "oh, Silas—is what you just said true? Because if it's true—won't you let it last after the water goes down? Won't you let Bitty keep his store?"

He looked down at me, frowning a little. One of the little yellow chicks in the coop got out between the bars just then, and was just falling on its nose when he caught it—I s'pose bill is more biologic, but it don't sound so dangerous—and he was tucking it back in, gentle, with its mother, while he answered me, testy:

"Lord, Calliope," he says, "a flood's a flood. Can't you keep things separate?"

"No, sir," I says, "I can't. Nor I don't believe the Lord can either."

Ain't it like things was arranged to happen in patterns, same as crystals? For it was just in them next two minutes that two things happened: The first was that a boy came riding over on his wheel from the telegraph office and give a telegram to Timothy. And Timothy opened it and waved it over his head, and come with it over to us:

"First contribution for the flood-suffers!" says he. "They telephoned the news over to Red Barns and listen at this: 'Put me down for Twenty-five dollars towards the flood folks food. Zachariah Roper.'"

I looked over to Timothy straight.

"Zachariah Roper," I says, "that owns the cement plant that some of the Flat folks got in the way of?"

Timothy jerked his shoulder distasteful. "The idear," says he, "of bringin' up business at a time like this."

With that I looked over at Silas, and I see him with the scarcest thing in the world for him—a little pinch of a smile on his face. Just for a minute he met my eyes. Then he looked down to get his hand a little farther away from where the old hen in the coop had been picking it.

And the other thing that happened was that up in front of me come running little Mrs. Bitty Marshall, and her eyes was full of tears.

"Oh, Mis' Marsh," she says, "what do you s'pose I done? I come off and left my lace curtain. I took it down first thing and pinned it up in a paper to bring. And then I come off and left it."

Before I could say a word Silas answered her:

"The water'll never get up that far, Mis' Marshall," he says, "don't you worry. Don't you worry one bit. But," says he, "if anything does happen to it, Mis' Marshall, I'll tell you now you can have as good a one as we've got in the store, *on me*. There now, you've had a present to-day a'ready!"

I guess she thanked him. I donno. All I remember is that pretty soon everybody begun to move towards town and I moved with 'em. And while we walked the whole thing kind of begun to take hold of me, what it meant, and things that had been coming to me all the morning came to me all together—and I wanted to chant 'em a chant, like Deborah (but pronounced Déborah when it's a relative). And I wanted to say:

"O Lord, look down on these eighty families, old and young and real young, that we've lived neighbor to all our lives, and yet we don't know half of 'em, either by name or by face, till now. Till now!

"And some of them we do know individual has showed up here today with a back-ground of families, wives and children they've got, just like anybody—Tippie that drives the dray and that's helped moved everybody; for twelve years he's moved my refrigerator out and my cook stove in, and vicious verses, as regular as Spring come and Autumn arrived; and there all the time he had a wife, with a cameo pin, and three little Tippies in plaid skirts and pink cheeks, asking everybody for a drink of water just like your own child, and one of 'em so nice that he might of been anybody's instead of just Tippie's.

"And Mamie Felt, that does up lace curtains of them that can afford to have 'em done up and dries 'em on a frame so's they hang straight and not like a waterfall with its expression blowing sideways, same as mine do—there's Mamie with her old mother and a cripple brother that we've never guessed about, and that she was doing for all the whole time.

"And Absalom Ricker's old mother, that's mourning bitter because she left her coral pin with a dog on behind on the Flats that her husband give it to her when they was engaged ... and we knew she was married, but not one of us had thought of her as human enough ever to have been engaged. And Mis' Haskitt with her new black dress, and Mis' Dole with her clean-ironed clothes bars, and Mis' Bitty Marshall with her baby and her little chickens and her lace curtain, and Bitty with his grocery store.

"Lord, we thank thee for letting us see them, and all the rest of 'em, *close up to.*

"We're glad that now just because the Mad river flowed into the homes that we ain't often been in or ever, if any, and drove up to us the folks that we've never thought so very much about, we're glad to get the feeling that I had when I heard our grocery-boy knew how to hand-carve wood and our mail man was announced to sing a bass solo, that we never thought they had any regular lives, separate from milk and mail.

"And let us keep that feeling, O Lord! Amen."

And I says right out of the fullness of the lump in my throat:

"Don't these folks seem so much more folks than they ever did before?"

Mis' Merriman that was near me, answered up:

"Why, of course," she says, "they're in trouble. Ain't you no compassion to you?"

"Some," says I, modest, "but where'd that compassion come from? It didn't just grow up now, did it?—like Abraham's gourd, or whoever it was that had one?"

"Why, no," she says irritable. "It's in us all, of course. But it takes trouble to bring it out."

"Why does it take trouble to bring it out?" I says and I looked ahead at us all a-streaming down Daphne Street, just like it was some nice human doings. "Why does it? Here's us all, and it only takes a minute to get us all going, with our hands in our pockets and lumps in our throats and our sympathy just as busy as it ever was for our little family in-four-walls affairs. Now," I says, "that love and sympathy, and them pockets and them throats are all here, just the same, day after day. What I want to know is, what are them things doing with themselves when nobody is in active trouble?"

And then I said my creed:

"O, when we get to working as hard to keep things from happening as we work when it's happened, won't living be fun?"

"Well, of course we couldn't prevent floods," says Mis' Merriman, "and them natural things."

"Shucks!" I says, simple. "If we knew as much about frosts and hurricanes as we do about comets—we'd show you. And do you think it's any harder to bank in a river than it is to build a subway—*if* there was the same money in it for the company?"

Just then the noon whistles blew—all of 'em together, round-house and brick-yard, so's you couldn't tell 'em apart; and the sun come shining down on us all, going along on Daphne Street. And all of a sudden Mis' Merriman looked over to me and smiled, and so I done to her, and I saw that our morning together and our feeling together had made us forget whatever there'd been between us to forget about. And I ain't ever in my life felt so kin to folks. I felt kinner than I knew I was.

That night, tired as I was, I walked over to see Mis' Sykes's night-blooming cereus—I don't see enough pretty things to miss one when I can get to it. And there, sitting on Mis' Sykes's front porch, with her shoes slipped off to rest her feet, was Mis' Holcomb-that-was-Mame Bliss.

"Mis' Sykes is out getting in a few pieces she washed out and forgot," says Mame, "and the Marshalls is all down town in a body sending a postal to say they're safe. Silas went too."

"The *Marshalls*!" says I. "Are they *here*?"

Mame nodded. "Silas asked 'em," she says. "Him and Bitty've been looking over grocery stock catalogues. Silas's been advising him some."

Mame and I smiled in concert. But whether the flood done it, or whether we done it—who cared?

"But, land, *you*, Mame!" I says. "I thought you—I thought Mis' Sykes...."

"I know it," says Mame. "I was. She did. But the first thing I knew to-day, there we was peeling potatoes together in the same pan, and we done it all afternoon. I guess we kind of forgot about our bad feeling...."

I set there, smiling in the dark.... I donno whether you know a village, along toward night, with the sky still pink, and folks watering their front lawns and calling to each other across the streets, and a little smell of bonfire smoke coming from somewheres? It was like that. And when Mis' Sykes come to tell us the flower was beginning to bloom, I says to myself that there was lots more in bloom in the world than any of us guessed.

THE PARTY

MIS' FIRE CHIEF MERRIMAN done her mourning like she done her house work—thorough. She was the kind of a housekeeper that looks on the week as made up of her duties, and the days not needing other names: Washday, Ironday, Mend-day, Bakeday, Freeday, Scrubday, and Sunday—that was how they went. With them nothing interfered without it was a circus or a convention or a company or the extra work on holidays. She kept house all over her, earnest; and when the Fire Chief died, that was the way she mourned.

When I say mourning I mean what you do besides the feeling bad part. She felt awful bad about her husband, but her mourning was somehow kind of separate from her grieving. Her grieving was done with her feelings, but her mourning was done more physical, like a diet. After the first year there was certain things she would and wouldn't do, count of mourning, and nothing could change them.

Weddings and funerals Mis' Fire Chief Merriman stayed true to. She would go to either. "Getting connect' or getting buried," she said, "them are both religious occasions, and they's somethin' so sad about either of 'em that they kind of fit in with weeds."

But she wouldn't go to a party if there was more than three or four to it, and not then if one of 'em was a stranger to her. And she wouldn't go to it unless it was to a house—picnics, where you sat around on the ground, she said, was too informal for them in mourning. Church meetings she went to, but not club meetings, except the Cemetery Improvement Sodality ones. It was like keeping track of etiquette to know what to do with Mis' Fire Chief Merriman.

"Seems though Aunt Hettie is more married now than she was when Uncle Eben was living," her niece use' to say.

It was on the little niece, Harriet Wells,—named for Mis' Chief and come to live with her a while before the Fire Chief died,—it was on her that Mis' Merriman's mourning etiquette fell the heaviest. Harriet was twenty and woman-pretty and beau-interested; and Amos More, that worked in Eppleby's feed store and didn't hev no folks, he'd been shining round the Merriman house some, and Harriet had been shining back, modest and low-wicked, but lit. He was spending mebbe a couple of evenings a week there and taking Harriet to sociables and entertainments some. But when the Fire Chief died Mis' Merriman set her foot down on Amos.

"I couldn't stand it," she says, "to hev a man comin' here that wasn't the Chief. I couldn't stand it to hev sparkin' an' courtin' goin' on all around me. An' if I should hev to hev a weddin' got ready for in this house—the dressmakin' an' like that—I believe I should scream."

So Amos he give up going there and just went flocking around by himself, and Harriet, she give all her time to her aunt, looking like a little lonesome candle that nothing answered back to. And Mis' Merriman's mourning flourished like a green bay tree.

It was into this state of affairs, more than a year after the Chief died, that Mis' Merriman's cousin's letter come. Mis' Merriman's cousin had always been one of them myth folks that every town has—the relations and friends of each other that is talked about and known about and heard from and even asked after, but that none of us ever sees. This cousin, Maria Carpenter, was one of our most intimate myths. Next to the Fire Chief himself, Mis' Merriman give the most of her time in conversation to her. She was real dressy—she used to send Mis' Merriman samples of her clothes and their trimmings, and we all felt real well acquainted and interested; and she was rich and busy and from the city, and the kind of a relation it done Mis' Merriman good to have connected with her, and her photograph with a real lace collar was on the parlor mantel. She had never been to Friendship Village, and we used to wonder why not.

And then she got the word that her cousin was actually flesh-an'-blood coming. I run in to Mis' Merriman's on my way home from town just after Harriet had brought her up the letter, and Mis' Merriman was all of a heap in the big chair.

"Calliope," she says, "the blow is down! Maria Carpenter is a-comin' Tuesday to stay till Friday."

"Well," I says, "ain't you glad, Mis' Fire Chief? Company ain't no great chore now the telephone is in," I says to calm her.

She looked up at me, sad, over her glasses.

"What good is it to have her come?" she says. "I can't show her off. There won't be a livin' place I can take her to. Nobody'll see her nor none of her clothes."

"It's too bad," I says absent, "it didn't happen so's you could give a company for Miss Carpenter."

Mis' Fire Chief burst out like her feelings overflowed themselves.

"It's what I've always planned," she says. "Many a night I've laid awake an' thought about the company I'd give when Maria come. An'

Maria never could come. An' now here is Maria all but upon me, an' the company can't be. I know she'll bring a dress, expectin' it. She knows it's past the first year, an' she'll think I'll feel free to entertain. I donno but I ought to telegraph her: *Pleased to see you but don't you expect a company.* Wouldn't that be more open an' aboveboard? Oh, dear!" Mis' Fire Chief says, rockin' in her chair that wouldn't rock, "I'm well an' the house is all in order an' I could afford a company if I didn't go in deep. But I couldn't bear to be to it. That's it, Calliope; I couldn't bear to be to it."

I remember Mis' Fire Chief kind of stopped then, like she thought of something; but I wasn't looking at her. I was watching Harriet Wells that was standing by the window a little to one side. And I see her lift her hand and give it a little wave and lay it on the glass like a signal to somebody. And all of a sudden I knew it was half past 'leven and that Amos More went home early to his dinner at the boarding house so's to get back at twelve-thirty, when Eppleby went for his, and that nine to ten it was Amos that Harriet was waving at. I knew it special and sure when Harriet turned back to the room with a nice little guilty look and a pink spot up high on both her cheeks. And something sort o' shut up in my throat. It seems so easy for folks to get married in this world, and here was these two not doing it.

All of a sudden Mis' Fire Chief Merriman jumped up on to her feet.

"Calliope Marsh," says she, "I've got a plan. I can do it, if you'll help me. Why can't I give a company," she says, "an' not come in the room? A hostess has to be in the kitchen most of the time anyway. Why can't I just stay there, an' leave Maria be in the parlor, an' me not be to the company at all?"

We talked it over, and neither of us see why not. Mis' Sykes, when she gives her series of companies, three in three days running, she often don't set foot in the parlor till after the refreshments are served. I remember once she was so faint she had to go back to the kitchen and eat her own supper, and we didn't say good-by to her at all, except as some of us that knew her best went and stuck our heads out the kitchen door. So with all us ladies—we done the same way when we entertained, so be we give 'em any kind of a lay-out.

"I won't say anything about the party bein' for Maria, one way or the other," she says; "I won't make a spread about it, nor much of an event. I'll just send out invites for a quiet time. Then when they come, you can stay in the room with Maria at first an' get her introduced. An' after that the party can go ahead on its own legs, just as well without me as with me. I could only fly in now an' then anyhow, an' talk to 'em snatchy, with my mind on the supper. Why ain't it just as good to stay right out of it altogether?"

We see it reasonable. And a couple of days before Maria Carpenter was expected, Mis' Fire Chief, she went to work, Harriet helping her, and she got her invitations out. They was on some black bordered paper and envelopes that Mis' Fire Chief had had for a mourning Christmas present an' had been saving. And they was worded real delicate, like Mis' Fire Chief done everything:

Mrs. Merriman, At Home, Thursday afternoon, Four o'clock Sharp, Thimbles. Six o'clock Supper. Walk right in past the bell.

It made quite a little stir in Friendship Village, because Mis' Merriman hadn't been anywheres yet. But everybody took it all right. And anyway, everybody was too busy getting ready, to bother much over anything else. It's quite a problem to know what to wear to a winter company in Friendship Village. Nobody entertains much of any in the winter—its a chore to get the parlor cleaned and het, and it's cold for 'em to lay off their things, and you can't think up much that's tasty for refreshments, being it's too cold to give 'em ice cream. Mis' Fire Chief was giving the party on the afternoon of Miss Carpenter's three o'clock arrival, in the frank an' public hope that somebody would dance around during her stay and give her a return invite out to tea or somewheres.

The morning of the day that was the day, there come a rap to my door while I was stirring up my breakfast, and there was Harriet Wells, bare-headed and a shawl around her, and looking summer-sweet in her little pink muslin dressing sacque that matched her cheeks and showed off her blue eyes.

"Aunt Hettie wants to know," she says, "whether you can't come over now so's to get an early start. She's afraid the train'll get in before we're ready for it."

"Land!" I says, "I know how she feels. The last company I give I got up and swep' by lamplight and had my cake all in the oven by 6 A.M. Come in while I eat my breakfast and I'll run right back with you and leave my dishes setting. How's your aunt standing it?" I ask' her.

"Oh, pretty well, thank you," says Hettie, "but she's awful nervous. She hasn't et for two days—not since the invitations went out o' the house—an' last night she dreamt about the Chief. That always upsets her an' makes her cross all next day."

"If she wasn't your aunt," I says, "I'd say, 'Deliver me from loving the dead so strong that I'm ugly to the living.' But she *is* your aunt and a good woman—so I'm mum as you please."

Hettie, she sighs some. "She *is* a good woman," she says, wistful; "but, oh, Mis' Marsh, they's some good women that it's terrible hard to live with," she says—an' then she choked up a little because she *had* said it. But I, and all Friendship Village, knew it for the truth. And we all wanted to be delivered from people that's so crazy to be moral and proper themselves, in life or in mourning, that they walk over everybody else's rights and stomp down everybody's feelin's. My eyes filled up when I looked at that poor, lonesome little thing, sacrificed like she was to Mis' Fire Chief's mourning spree.

"Hettie," I says, "Amos More goes by here every morning about now on his way to his work. When he goes by this morning, want to know what I'm going to tell him?"

"Yes'm," says Hettie, simple, blushing up like a pink lamp shade when you've lit the lamp.

"I'm a-goin' to tell him," says I, "that I'm going to ask Eppleby Holcomb to let him off for a couple of ours or so this morning, an' a couple more this afternoon. I want he should come over to Mis' Fire Chief's an' chop ice an help turn freezer." (We was going to feed 'em ice cream even if it was winter.) "I'm getting too old for such fancy jobs myself, and you ain't near strong enough, and Mis' Chief, I know how she'll be. She won't reco'nize her own name by nine o'clock."

While I was finding out what cocoanut and raisins and such they'd got in stock, along come Amos More, hands hanging loose like he'd lost his grip on something. I called to him, and pretended not to notice Harriet's little look into the clock-door looking-glass, and when he come in I 'most forgot what I'd meant to say to him, it was so nice to see them two together. I never see two more in love with every look of each other's.

"Why, Harriet!" says Amos, as if saying her name was his one way of breathing.

"Good mornin', Amos," Harriet says, rose-pink and looking at the back of her hand.

Amos just give me a little nice smile, and then he didn't seem to know I was in the room. He went straight up to her and caught a-hold of the fringe of her shawl.

"Harriet," he says, "how long have I got to go on livin' on the sight of you through that dinin'-room window? Yes, livin'. It's the only time I'm alive all day long—just when I see you there, signalin' me—an' when I know you ain't forgot. But I can't go on this way—I can't, I can't."

"What can I do—what can I do, Amos?" she says, faint.

"Do? Chuck everything for me—if you love me enough," says Amos, neat as a recipe.

"I owe Aunt Hettie too much," says Hettie, firm; "I ain't that kind—to turn on her ungrateful."

"I know it. I love you for that too," says Amos, "I love you on account of everything you do. And I tell you I can't live like this much longer."

"Well said!" I broke in, brisk; "I can help you over this day anyhow. You go on down-town, Amos, and get the stuff on this list I've made out, and then you come on up to Mis' Fire Chief's. We need a man and we need you. I'll fix it with Eppleby."

They wasn't any need to explain to Mis' Fire Chief. She was so excited she didn't know whether she was a-foot or a-horseback. When Amos got back with the things I'd sent for she didn't seem half to sense it was him I was sending out in the woodshed to chop ice. She didn't hev her collar on nor her shoes buttoned, and she wasn't no more use in that kitchen than a dictionary.

"Oh, Calliope," she says, in a sort of wail, "I'm so nervous!"

"You go and set down, Mis' Fire Chief," says I, "and button up your shoes. I've got every move of the morning planned out," says I, "so be you don't interrupt me."

Of course it was her party and all, but they's some hostesses you hev to lay a firm holt of, if you're the helper and expect the party to come off at all. And I never see any living hostess more upset than was Mis' Fire Chief. She give all the symptoms—not of a company, but of coming down with something.

"Oh, Calliope," says she, "everything's against me. I donno," she says, "but it's a sign from the Chief in his grave that I'm actin' against his wishes an' opposite to what widows should. The wood is green—hear it siss an' sizzle in that stove an' hold back its heat from me. The cistern is dry—we've hed to pump water to the neighbors. Not a hen has cackled this livelong mornin' in the coop. The milkman couldn't only leave me three quarts instead of four, though ordered ahead. An' I feel like death—I feel like death," says she, "part on account of the Chief—ain't it like he was speakin' his disapprovin' in all these little minor ways?—an' part because I know I'm comin' down with a hard cold an' I'd ought to be in bed all lard an' pepper this livin' minute. Oh, dear me! An' Maria all but upon me. I don't know how I'll ever get through this day."

"Mis' Fire Chief," says I, "you go and lay down and try to get some rest."

"No, Calliope," says she, "the beds is all ready for the company to lay their hats off, an' the lounge pillows has been beat light on the line."

"Well," says I, "go off an' take a walk."

"Not without I walk to the cemetery," says she, "an' that I couldn't bear. Not to-day."

"Well," says I, "then you let me put a wet cloth over your head and eyes, and you set still and stop talkin'. You'll be wore to a thread," says I.

And that was what I done to her, expecting that if she didn't keep still I'd bake the ice cream and freeze the cake and lose my own head entire.

Out in the shed I'd set Amos to cracking ice, and Harriet to cracking nuts, with a flatiron and a hammer. And pretty soon I stepped along to see how things was going. Land, land, it was a pretty sight! They was both working away, but Amos was looking down at her more'n to his work, and Harriet was looking up at him like he was all of it—and the whole air was pleasant with something sweeter than could be named. So I left them two alone, well knowing that I could manage a company sole by myself yet a while, no matter how much courting and mourning was going on all around me.

And everything went fine, in spite of Mis' Fire Chief's looking like death in the rocker, with a wet rag on her brow.

But she kept lifting up one corner and giving directions.

"No pink frostin', Calliope, you know," she says, "only white. An' no colored flowers—only white ones. You'll have to write the place cards—my hand shakes so I don't dare trust myself. But I'll cut up the ribbin for the sandwiches—I can do that much," says she.

The place cards was mourning ones, with broad black edges, and the ribbin to tie up the sandwiches was black too. And the centerpiece was one Mis' Fire Chief and Hettie hed been up early that morning making—it was a set piece from the Chief's funeral, a big goblet, turned bottom side up, done in white geraniums with "He is Near" in purple everlastings. The table was going to look real tasty, Mis' Fire Chief thought, all in black and white so—with little sprays of willow laid around on the cloth instead of ferns.

"I've done the best I could," she said, solemn, "to make the occasion do honor to Maria an' pay reverence to the Chief."

I had just finally persuaded her to go up-stairs and look the chambers over and then try to take a little rest somewheres around, when Amos come to the shed door to tell me the freezer wouldn't turn no more, and was it broke or was the cream froze. And Mis' Fire Chief, seeing him coming in the shed way, seemed to sense for the first time that he was there.

"Amos More," says she, "what you doin' here?"

"I ask' him," says I, hasty; "I had to have his help about the ice."

She covered her eyes with one hand. "Courtin' an' entertainin' goin' on in the Chief's house," she said, "an' him only just gone from us!"

"Well," s'I, "I've got to have *some* man's help out here this afternoon—why not Amos's?"

"Oh," says Mis' Merriman, "you're all against me but the Chief, an' him helpless."

"The Chief," says I, "was always careful of your health. You'll make yourself sick taking on so, Mis' Fire Chief," I told her. "You go and put flowers in the chambers and leave the rest to me. Put your mind," I told her, "on the surprise you've got for your guests that's comin'—Maria Carpenter here and all! Besides," I couldn't help sticking in, "I donno as Amos is cold poison."

So we got her off up-stairs.

Maria Carpenter's train was due at 3:03, so she was just a-going to have the right time to get ready when the afternoon would begin, because in Friendship Village "sharp four" means four o'clock. I had left the sandwiches to make last thing, and I come back from my dinner towards three and tiptoes through the house so's not to disturb Mis' Fire Chief if she was resting, and I went into the pantry and begun cutting and spreading bread. I hadn't been there but a little while before the stair door into the kitchen opened and I heard Hettie come down, humming a little. But before I could sing out to her, the woodshed door opened too, and in come Amos that had been out putting more salt in the freezer.

"Hettie!" he says in a low voice, and I see she prob'ly hed on her white muslin and was looking like angels, and more. And—"I won't," says Amos, then—"I won't—though I can hardly keep my hands off from you—dear."

"It don't seem right even to have you call me 'dear,'" says Hettie, sad.

Amos burst right out. "It is right—it is *right!*" says he. "They can't nobody make me feel 'dear' is wicked, not when it means as dear as you are to me. Hettie," Amos says, "sit down here a minute."

"Not us. Not together," says Hettie, nervous.

"Yes!" says Amos, commanding, "I don't know when I'll see you again. Set down here, by me."

And by the little stillness, I judged she done so. And I says this: "Them poor things ain't had ten minutes with each other in over a year, and if they know I'm here, that'll spoil this time. I'd better stay where I am, still, with my thoughts on my sandwiches." And that was what I done. But I couldn't—I *couldn't*—and neither could most anyone—of helped a word or two leaking through the pantry door *and* the sandwich thoughts.

"I just wanted to pretend—for a minute," Amos said, "that this was our house. An' our kitchen. An' that we was settin' here side of the stove an' belonged."

"Oh, Amos," said Hettie, "it don't seem right to pretend that way with Aunt Hettie's stove—an' her feelin' the way she does."

"Yes, it is right," says Amos, stout. "Hettie! Don't you see? She *don't* feel that way. She's just nervous with grievin', an' it comes out like that. She don't care—really. At least not anything like the way she thinks she does. Now don't let's think about her, Hettie—dearest! Think about now. An' let's just pretend for a minute it was then. You know—*then*!"

"Well," says Hettie, unwilling,—and yet, oh, so willing,—"if it *was* then, what would you be sayin'?"

"I'd be sayin' what I say now," says Amos, "an' what I'll say to the end o' time: that I love you so much that the world ain't the world without you. But I want to hear *you* say somethin'. What would you be sayin', Hettie, if it was *then*?"

I knew how she dimpled up as she answered—Hettie's dimples was like the wind had dented a rose leaf.

"I'd prob'ly be sayin'," says Hettie, "Amos, you ain't filled the water pail. An' I'll have to have another armful o' kindlin'."

"Well," says Amos, "but then when I'd brought 'em. What would you say then?"

"I'd say, 'What do you want for dinner?'" said Hettie, demure. But even this was too much for Amos.

"An' then we'd cook it," he says, almost reverent. "Oh, Hettie—don't it seem like heaven to think of us seein' to all them little things—together?"

I loved Hettie for her answer. Coquetting is all right some of the time; but—some of the time—so is real true talk.

"Yes," she says soft, "it does. But it seems like earth too—*an' I'm glad of it.*"

"Oh, Hettie," says Amos, "marry me. Don't let's go on like this."

"Dear," says Hettie, all solemn,—and forgetting that "dear" was such a wicked word,—"dear, I'd marry you this afternoon if it wasn't for Aunt Hettie's feelin's. But I can't hurt her—I can't," she says.

Well, just then the door bell rung, and Hettie she flew to answer it, and Amos he lit back to the woodshed and went to chopping more ice like life lay all that way. And I was just coming out of the butt'ry with a pan of thin sandwiches ready for the black ribbins, when I heard a kind of groan and a scuffle, and down-stairs come Mis' Fire Chief Merriman, and all but fell into the kitchen. She had something in her hand.

"Calliope—Calliope Marsh," says she, all wailing like a bereavement, "Cousin Maria has fell an broke her wrist, an' she ain't comin' *at all!*"

I stood still, real staggered. I see what it meant to Mis' Merriman—invites all out, Cousin Maria for surprise and hostess in one, Mis' Merriman not figgering on appearing at all, account of the Chief, and the company right that minute on the way.

"What'll I do—what'll I *do?*" cries Mis' Merriman, sinking down on the bottom step in her best black with the crêpe cuffs. "Oh," she says, "it's a judgment upon me. I'll hev to turn my guests from my door. I'll be the laughing-stock," says she, wild.

And just then, like the trump of judgment to her, we heard the front door shut, and the first folks to come went marching up the stairs. And at the same minute Amos come in from the shed with the dasher out of the second freezer, and Hettie's eyes run to him like he was their goal and their home. And then I says:

"Mis' Fire Chief. Leave your company come in. Serve 'em the food of your house, just like you've got it ready. Stay back in the kitchen and don't go in the parlor and do it all just like you'd planned. And in place of Maria Carpenter and the surprise you'd meant," says I, "give 'em another surprise. Leave Hettie and Amos be married in your parlor, like they want to be and like all Friendship Village wants to see 'em. Couldn't nothing be sweeter."

Mis' Merriman stared up to me, and set and rocked.

"A weddin'," she says, "a weddin' in the parlor where the very last gatherin' was the funeral of the Chief? It's sacrilege—sacrilege!" she says, wild.

"Mis' Merriman," I says, simple, "what do you reckon this earth is about? What," says I, "is the purpose the Lord God Most High created it for out of nothing? As near as I can make out," I told her, "and I've give the matter some study, He's got a purpose hid way deep in His heart, and way deep in the hearts of us all has got to be the same purpose, or we might just as well, and a good sight better, be dead. And a part of that purpose is to keep His world a-going, and that can't be done, as I see it, by looking back over our shoulders to the dead that's gone, however dear, and forgetting the living that's all around us, yearning and thirsting and passioning for their happiness. And a part of His purpose is to put happiness into this world, so's people can brighten up and hearten out and do the work of the world like He meant 'em to. And you, Mis' Merriman," says I, plain, "are a-holding back from both them purposes of God's, and a-doing your best to set 'em to naught."

Mis' Merriman, she looked up kind of dazed from where she was a-sitting. "I ain't never supposed I was livin' counter to the Almighty," she says, some stiff.

"Well," says I, "none of us supposes that as much as we'd ought to. And my notion, and the notion of most of Friendship Village, it's just what you're doing, Mis' Fire Chief," says I,—"in some respec's."

"Oh, even if I wasn't, I don't want to be the laughin'-stock to-day," says she, weak, and beginning to cry.

"Hettie and Amos," says I, then, for form's sake, "if Mis' Merriman agrees to this, do you agree?"

"Yes! Oh, *yes*!" says Amos, like the organ and the benediction and the Amen, all rolled into one.

"Yes," says Hettie, shy as a rose, but yet like a rose nodding on its stalk, positive.

"And you, Mis' Fire Chief?" says I.

She nodded behind her hands that covered up her face. "I don't know what to do," says she, faint. "Go on ahead—all of you!"

My, if we didn't have to fly around. They wasn't no time for dress changing. Hettie was in white muslin and Amos in every-day, but it was all right because she was Hettie and because he looked like a king in anything. And they was so many last things to do that none of us thought of dress anyhow. It was four o'clock by then, and folks had been stomping in "past the bell" and marching up-stairs and laying off their things—being as everybody knows what's what in Friendship Village and don't hev to be told where to go, same as some—till, judging by the sound, they had all got there and was clacking in the parlor, and Mis' Fire Chief's party had begun. And Mis' Fire Chief herself revived enough to offer to tie the ribbins around the sandwiches.

"My land!" I says, "we can't do that. We can't have black ribbin round the wedding sandwiches."

But Hettie, she broke in, sweet and dignified, and before her aunt could say a word. "Yes, we can," she says, "yes, we can. I ain't superstitious, same as some. Uncle's centerpiece an' his willow on the tablecloth an' his blackribbin sandwiches," says she, "is goin' to stay just the way they are, weddin' or no weddin'," says she. "Ain't they, Amos?" she ask' him.

"You bet you," says Amos, fervent, just like he would have agreed to anything under heaven that Hettie said. And Mis' Merriman, she looked at 'em then, grateful and even resigned. And time Amos had gone and got back with the license and the minister we were all ready.

They sent me in to sort of pave the way. I slips in through the hall and stood in the door a minute wondering how I'd tell 'em. There they all was, setting sewing and rocking and gossiping, contented as if they had a hostess in every room. And not one of 'em suspecting. Oh, I loved 'em one and all, and I loved the way they was all *used* to each other, and talking natural about crochet patterns and recipes for oatmeal cookies and what's good to keep hands from chapping—not one of 'em putting on or setting their best foot forwards or trying to act their best, same as they might with company, but just being themselves, natural and forgetting. And I was glad, deep down in my heart, that Maria Carpenter hadn't come near. Not glad that she had broke her wrist, of course—but that she hadn't come near. And when I stepped out to tell 'em what was going to happen, I was so glad in my throat that I couldn't say a word only just—

"Friends—listen to me. What do you *s'pose* is goin' to happen? Oh, they can't none of you guess. So look. Look!"

Then I threw open the dining-room door and let 'em in—Hettie and Amos, with Doctor June. And patterns and recipes and lotions all just simmered down into one surprised and glad and loving buzz of wonder. And then Hettie and Amos were married, and the world begun all over again, Garden of Eden style.

There is one little thing more to tell. When the congratulations was most over, the dining-room door creaked a little bit, and Amos, that was standing by it, whirled around and see Mis' Fire Chief Merriman peeking through the crack to her guests. And Amos swung open the door wide, and he grabbed her by the arm, and though she hung back with all her strength

Amos pulled her right straight into the room and kissed her, there before them all.

"*Aunt* Hettie," he says to her, ringing, "*Uncle*—Hettie's uncle an' mine an' your husband,—wouldn't want you stayin' out there in the dinin'-room to-day on account o' him!"

And when we all crowded around her, greeting her like guests should greet a hostess and like dear friends should greet dear friends, Mis' Fire Chief she wipes her eyes, and she left 'em shake her hands; and though she wasn't all converted, it was her and not me that ask' 'em please to walk out into the dining-room and eat the lunch that was part wedding and part in memory of the Chief.

THE BIGGEST BUSINESS

I DONNO whether you've ever lived in a town that's having a boom? That's being a boom town, as they call it? There ain't any more boom to Friendship Village than there is to a robin building a nest. There ain't any more boom to Friendship Village than there is to growth. We just go along and go along, and behave ourselves like the year does: Little spurt of Spring now and then, when two-three folks build new houses and we get a new side-walk or two or buy a new sprinkling cart. Little dead time, here and there, when the tobacco or pickle factory closes down to wait for more to grow, and when somebody gets most built and boards up the windows till something else comes in to go on with. But most of the time Friendship Village keeps on pretty even, like the year, or the potato patch, or any of them common, growing things.

But now over to Red Barns it ain't so. Red Barns is eight miles away, and from the beginning the two towns sort of set with their backs to each other, and each give out promiscuous that the other didn't have a future. But, same time, the two towns looked out of the corners of their eyes enough to set quite a few things going for each other unconscious: Red Barns got a new depot, and Friendship Village instantly petitioned for one. Friendship Village set aside a little park, and Red Barns immediately appropriated for one, with a little edge more ground. Red Barns got a new post office, and Friendship Village started out for a new library. And so on. Just like a couple of boys seeing which could swim out farthest.

Then all of a sudden the Interurban come through Red Barns and left Friendship Village setting quiet out in the meadows eight miles from the track. And of course after that Red Barns shot ahead—Eppleby Holcomb said that on a still night you could hear Red Barns chuckle. Pretty soon a little knitting factory started up there, and then a big tobacco factory. And being as they had three motion-picture houses to our one, and band concerts all Summer instead of just through July, the folks in Silas Sykes's Friendship Village Corn Canning Industry and in Timothy Toplady's Enterprise Pickle Manufactory began to want to go over to Red Barns to work. Two left from Eppleby Holcomb's Dry Goods Emporium. Even the kitchens of the few sparse ones that kept hired help begun to suffer. And the men begun to see that what was what had got to be helped to be something else—same as often happens in commercial circles.

Things was about to this degree when Spring come on. I donno how it is with other people, but with me Spring used to be the signal to run as far as I could from the place I was in, in the hopes, I guess, of getting close up to all outdoors. I used to want to run along country paths all squshy with water, and hang over a fence to try to tell whether it's a little quail or a big meadowlark in the sedge; I wanted to smell the sweet, soft-water smell that Spring rain has. I wanted to watch the crust of the earth move because May was coming up through the mold. I wanted to climb a tree and be a bud. And one morning I got up early bent on doing all these things, and ended by poking round my garden with a stick to see what was coming up—like you do. It was real early in the morning—not much after six—and Outdoors looked surprised—you know that surprised look of early morning, as if the day had never thought of being born again till it up and happened to it? And I had got to the stage of hanging over the alley fence, doing nothing, when little David Beach come by. He was eating a piece of bread, and hurrying.

"Morning, David," I sings out. "Where's your fish-pole?"

He stopped running and stopped biting and looked up at me. And then he laughed, sharp and high up.

"Fish-pole!" says he.

"Is it swimming, then?" I says. And then I felt sick all over. For I remembered that David had gone to work in Silas Sykes's canning factory.

"Oh, David," I patched it up. "I forgot. You're a man now."

At that he put back his thin little shoulders, and stuck out his thin little chest, and held up his sharp little chin. And he said:

"Yup. I'm a man now. I get $2.50 a week, *now*."

"Whew!" says I. "When do you bank your first million?"

He grinned and broke into a run again. "I'm docked if I'm late," he shouts back.

I looked after him. It didn't seem ten days since he was born. And here he was, of the general contour of a clay pipe, going to work. His father had been crippled in the factory, his mother was half sick, and there were three younger than David, and one older.

"Kind of nice of Silas to give David a job," I thought. "I don't suppose he's worth much to him, he's so little."

And that was all I thought, being that most of us uses our heads far more frequent to put hats on than for any other purpose.

Right after breakfast that morning I took a walk down town to pick out my vegetables before the flies done 'em too much violence in Silas

Sykes's store window. And out in front of the store, I come on Silas himself, sprinkling his wilted lettuce.

The minute I see Silas, I knew that something had happened to make him pleased with himself. Not that Silas ain't always pleased with himself. But that day he looked extra-special self-pleased.

"Hello, Calliope," he says, "you're the very one I want to help me."

That surprised me, but, thinks I, I've asked Silas to do so many things he ain't done that I've kind of wore grooves in the atmosphere all around him; and I guess he's took to asking me first when he sees me, for fear I'll come down on to him with another request. So I followed him into the post-office store where he motioned me with his chin, and this was what he says:

"Calliope," says he, "how'd you like to help me do a little work for this town?"

I must just of stared at Silas. I can keep from looking surprised, same as the best, when a neighbor comes down on to me, with her eyebrows up over a piece of news—and I always do, for I do hate to be expected to play up to other folks's startled eyebrows. But with these words of Silas's I give in and stared. For of some eight, nine, ten plans that I'd approached him with to the same end, he had turned down all them, and all me.

"With who?" says I.

"For who?" says he. "Woman, do you realize that taking 'em all together, store and canning factory combined, I've got forty-two folks a-working for me?"

"Well!" says I. "Quite a family."

"Timothy Toplady's got twelve employees," he goes on, "and Eppleby's got seven in the store. That's sixty-one girls and women and then ... er...."

"Children," says I, simple.

"Young folks," Silas says, smooth. "Sixty-one of 'em. Ain't that pretty near a club, I'd like to know?"

"Oh," I says, "a club. A club! And do them sixty-one want to *be* a club, Silas?"

Silas scowled. "What you talking?" he says. "Of course they want all you'll do for 'em. Well, now: Us men has been facing this thing, and it's so plain that even a woman must see it: Friendship Village is going to empty itself out into Red Barns, same as a skin, if this town don't get up and do something."

"True," says I, attentive. "Even a woman can take in that much, Silas, if you put it right before her, and lead her up to it, and point it out to her and," says I, warming up to it, "put blinders on her so's not to distract her attention from the real fact in hand."

"What you talking?" says Silas. "I never saw a woman yet that could keep on any one subject no more than a balloon. Well, now, what I thought was this: I thought I'd up and go around with a paper, and see how much everybody'd give, and we'd open an Evening Club somewheres, for the employees—folks's old furniture and magazines and books and some games—and give 'em a nice time. Here," says Silas, producing a paper from behind the cheese, "I've gone into this thing to the tune of Fifty Dollars. Fifty Dollars. And I thought," says he direct, "that you that's always so interested in doing things for folks, might put your own name down, and might see some of the other ladies too. And I could report it to our Commercial club meeting next Friday night. *After* the business session."

I looked at him, meditative.

"If it's all the same to you, Silas," I says, "I'll take this paper and go round and see some of these sixty-one women and girls, instead."

Silas kind of raised up his whole face and left his chin hanging, idle.

"See them women and girls?" says he, some resembling a shout. "What have they got to do with it, I'd like to know?"

"Oh," says I, "ain't it some their club too, Silas? I thought the whole thing was on their account."

Silas used his face like he'd run a draw string down it.

"Women," he says, "dum women. Their minds ain't any more logical than—than floor-sweepings with the door open. Didn't I just tell you that the thing was going to be done for the benefit of Friendship Village and to keep them folks interested in it?"

"Well, but," I says, "ain't them folks some Friendship Village too?"

"What's that got to do with it?" shouts Silas. "Of course they are. Of course we want to help 'em. But *they* ain't got anything to do with it. All they got to do with it is to be helped!"

"Is it!" I says. "Is that all, Silas?" And while he was a-gathering himself up to reply, I picked up the subscription paper. "It can't do 'em no harm," I says, "to tell 'em about this. Then if any of 'em is thinking of leaving, it may hold on to 'em till we get a start. If it's all the same to you, I'll just run around and see 'em to-day. Mebbe they might help—who knows?"

"You'll bawl the whole thing up," says Silas. "I wish't I'd kep' my mouth shut."

"Well," I says, "you'd ought to know by this time that I ain't any great hand to do things *for* folks, Silas. I like to do 'em *with* 'em."

Silas was starting in to wave both arms when somebody come in for black molasses. And he says to me:

"Well, go on ahead. You'll roon my whole idea—but go on ahead and see how little hurt you can do. I've got to have some lady-help from somewheres," says he, frank.

"Lady-help," thinks I, a-proceeding down the street. "Lady-help. That's me. Kind of auxiliarating around. A member of the General Ladies' Aid Society. Lady-help. Ain't it a grand feeling?"

I went straight to Abigail Arnold that keeps the Home Bakery. Abigail lives in the Bakery, and I donno a nicer, homier place in town. She didn't make the mistake of putting up lace curtains in the store, to catch the dust.... I always wonder when the time'll come that we'll be content not to have any curtains to any windows in the living rooms of this earth, but just to let the boughs and the sun and the day smile in on us, like loving faces. Fade things? Fade 'em? I wonder they didn't think of that when they made the sun, and temper it down to keep the carpets good.... Sometimes I dream of a house on a hill, with meadows of grass and the line of the sky and the all-day sun for neighbors, and not a thing to say to 'em: "Keep out. You'll fade me." But, "Come in. You'll feed me."

Well, Abigail Arnold was making her home-made doughnuts that morning, and the whole place smelled like when you was twelve years old, and struck the back stoop, running, about the time the colander was set on the wing of the stove, heaped up with brown, sizzling, doughnut-smelling doughnuts.

"Set right down," she says, "and have one." And so I done. And for a few minutes Silas and Red Barns and Friendship Village and the industrial and social relations of the entire country slipped away and was sunk in that nice-tasting, crumpy cake. Ain't it wonderful—well, we'd ought not to bother to go off into that; but sometimes I could draw near to the whole human race just thinking how every one of us loves a fresh doughnut, et in somebody's kitchen. It's a sign and symbol of how alike we are—and I donno but it means something, something big.

But with the last crumb I come back to commerce.

"Abigail," I says, "Silas wants to start a club for his and Timothy's and Eppleby's employees."

"Huh!" says Abigail, sticking her fork down in the kettle. "What's the profit? Ain't I getting nasty in my old age?" she adds solemn. "I meant, Go on. Tell me about it."

I done so, winding up about the meeting to be held the coming Friday in Post-Office Hall, at which Silas was to report on the progress of the club, after the business session. And she see it like I see it: That a club laid on to them sixty-one people had got to be managed awful wise—or what was to result would be considerable more like the stuff put into milk to preserve it than like the good, rich, thick cream that milk knows how to *give*, so be you treat it right.

Abigail said she'd help—she's one of them *new* women—oh, I ain't afraid of the word—she's one of them new women that catches fire at a big thing to be done in the world just as sure as another kind of woman flares up when her poor little pride is hurt. I've seen 'em both in action, and so have you. And we made out a list—in between doughnuts—of them sixty-one women and girls and children that was working in Friendship Village, and we divided up the list according to which of us was best friends with which of 'em—you know that's a sort of thing you can't leave out in the sort of commercial enterprise we was embarking on—and we agreed to start out separate, right after supper, and see what turned out to be what.

I went first to see Mary Beach, little David Beach's sister. They lived about half a mile from the village on a little triangle of land that had been sold off from both sides and left because it was boggy. They had a little drab house, with thick lips. David's mother set outside the door with a big clothes-basketful of leggings beside her. She was a strong, straight creature with a mass of gray hair, and a way of putting her hands on her knees when she talked, and eyes that said: "I know and I think," and not "I'm sure I can't tell," like so many eyes are built to represent. Mary that I'd come to see might have been a person in a portrait—she was that kind of girl. And little David was there, laying sprawled out on the floor taking a clock to pieces and putting the items in a pie-tin.

"You won't care," says Mis' Beach, "if I keep on with the leggings?"

"Leggings?" says I.

She nodded to the basket. "It's bad pairs," she said. "They leave me catch up the dropped stitches."

"How much do they give you?" says I, brutal. If it had been Silas Sykes I'd never have dreamt of asking him how much anybody give him for anything. But—well, sometimes we hound folks and hang folks and ask folks questions, merely because they're poor.

"Six cents a dozen," she says.

I remember they had a fly-paper on the window sill, and the caught flies and the uncaught ones whirred and buzzed. I can see the room: The floor that sagged, the walls that cracked, the hot, nameless smell of it. And in it a woman with the strength and the figure of a race that hasn't got here yet, and three children—one of them beautiful, and David, taking a clock to pieces and putting it together again, without ever having been taught. You know all about it—and so did I. And while I set there talking with her, I couldn't keep my mind on anything else but that hole of a home, and the three splendid beings chained there, like folks in a bad dream. Someway I never get used to it, and I know I never shall. It makes me feel as if I was looking on the inside of a table spoon and seeing things twisted, and saying: "Already such things can't be. Already they sound old and false—like thumbscrews!"

And the worst of it was, David's mother was so used to it. She was so bitter used to it. And oh—don't things turn round in the world? A few years before if somebody like me had gone to see her, I'd of been telling her to be resigned, and to make the best of her lot, and trying to give her to understand that the Lord had meant it personal. And instead, when she said she was doing nice, I longed to say to her:

"No, no, Mis' Beach! Don't you make that mistake. You ain't doing nice. As long as you think you are, this world is being held back. It's you that's got to help folks to know that you *aren't* doing nice. And to make folks wonder why."

But I didn't say it to her. I s'pose I haven't got that far—yet.

She said she'd like to come to the club that Silas proposed, and Mary, she said she'd come. They didn't question much about it—they merely accepted it and said they'd come. And I went out into the April after-supper light, with a bird or two twittering sleepy, and an orange and lemon and water-melon sunset doing its best to attract my attention, and I says out loud to April in general:

"A club. A club. So we're going to help that house with a club."

Then I stopped to Mis' Cripps's boarding house. Mis' Cripps's boarding house faces the railroad tracks, and I never went by there without seeing her milk bottles all set out on her porch, indelicate, like some of the kitchen lining showing. Bettie Forkaw and Libbie Collins and Rose Miller and Lizzie Lane, pickle factory girls, lived there. They were all home, out on the smoky porch, among the milk bottles, laughing and talking and having a grand time. They had sleeves above their elbows and waists turned in at the throat with ruffles of cheap lace, and hair braided in bunches over their ears and dragged low on their foreheads, and they had long, shiney beads round their necks, and square, shiney buckles on their low shoes. Betty was pretty and laughed loud and had uncovered-looking eyes. Libbie was big and strong and still. Rose was thin, and she had less blood and more bones than anybody I ever see. And Lizzie—Lizzie might have been a freshman in any college you might name. She'd have done just as good work in figures as she did in pickles—only cucumbers come her way and class-rooms didn't.

"Hello, girls," I says, "how are you to-night? Do you want to be a club?"

"To do what?" says they.

"Have a good time," says I. "Have music—eat a little something—dance—read a little, maybe. And ask your friends there. A *club*, you know."

After we'd talked it over, all four of 'em said yes, they wished they had some place to go evenings and wouldn't it be fine to have some place give to 'em where they could go. I didn't discuss it over with 'em at all—but I done the same thing I'd done before, and that I cannot believe anybody has the right to ask, no matter how rich the questioner or how poor the questionee.

"Girls," I says, "you all work for Silas Sykes, don't you? How much do you get a week?"

They told me ready enough: Five and Six Dollars apiece, it was.

"Gracious," I says, "how can you use up so much?" And they laughed and thought it was a joke. And I went along to the next place—and my thoughts come slowly gathering in from the edges of my head and formed here and there in kind of clots, that got acted on by things I begun to see was happening in my town, just as casual as meat bills and grocery bills—just as casual as school bells and church bells.

For the next two days I went to see them on my list. And then nights I'd go back and sit on my porch and look over to Red Barns that was posting itself as a nice, hustling, up-to-date little town, with plenty of business opportunities. And then I'd look up and down Friendship Village that was getting ready for its Business meeting in Post-Office Hall on Friday night, and trying its best to keep up with its "business reputation." And then I'd go on to some more homes of the workers that was keeping up their share in the commercial life of Friendship Village. And then my thoughts would bring up at Silas's club house, with the necessary old furniture and magazines and games laid out somewheres, tasty. And the little clots of thought in my brain somehow stuck there. And I couldn't think through them, on to what was what.

Then something happened that put a little window in the side of what was the matter with Silas's plan. And I begun to see light.

The second night I was sitting on my porch when I heard my back gate slam. My back gate has a chain for a spring, weighted with a pail of stones, and when it slams the earth trembles, and I have time to get my hands out of the suds or dough or whatever; and it's real handy and practical. This time there come trotting round my house David Beach. My, my but he was a nice little soul. He had bright eyes, that looked up quick as a rabbit's. And a smile that slipped on and off, swift as a frisking squirrel. And he had little darting movements, like a chipmunk's. There was something wild about him, like the wind. Silas's pickle factory did seem a queer place for us to have put him.

"Look, Miss Marsh!" he says. And he was holding out his clock. "I got it all together," he says, "and it'll go. And it'll go right."

"Did you now?" I says. And it was true. He had. It did. That little alarm clock was ticking away like a jeweller-done job.... Yes, Silas's pickle factory did seem a queer place for us to have put him.

When the little lad had gone off through the dusk, with his clock under his arm, I looked down the street after him. And I thought of this skill of his. And then I thought of the $2.50 a week Silas was giving him for shelling corn. And then I thought of this club that was to keep him and the rest of 'em contented. And I begun to see, dim, just the particular kinds of fools we was making of ourselves.

There was yet one thing more happened that wasn't so much a window as a door. The next night was to be the Business Men's meeting, and just before supper I went to pay my last visit on my list. It was out to the County House to see the superintendent's niece that had just resigned from Eppleby's store, and that they were afraid was going to Red Barns to work.

The County House. Ain't that a magnificent name? Don't we love to drape over our bones and our corpses some flying banner of a word like sarcophagus? The County House sets on a hill. A hill is a grand place for a County House. "Look at me," the County House can say, "I'm what a beneficent and merciful people can do for its unfit." And I never go by one that I don't want to shout back at it: "Yes. Look at you. You're our biggest confession of our biggest sham. What right have we, in Nineteen Hundred Anything, to have any unfit left?"

Right in front of the County House is a cannon. I never figured out the fitness of having a cannon there—in fact, I never can figure out the fitness of having a cannon anywhere. But one thing I've always noticed: When public buildings and such do have cannon out in front of them, they're always pointing *away* from the house. Never toward the house. Always going to shoot somebody else. That don't seem to me etiquette. If we must keep cannon for ornament, aren't we almost civilized enough to turn 'em around?

Seems the superintendent's niece wasn't going to Red Barns at all— she'd merely resigned to be married and had gone to town to buy things—a part of being married which competes with the ceremony, neck and neck, for importance. In the passageway, the matron called me in the office. She was a tall, thick woman with a way of putting her hand on your back to marshal you, as mothers do little children in getting them down an aisle. Yes, she was a marshaling woman.

"Look here," says the matron, proud.

They'd put a glass case up in the office and it was all hung with work—crocheted things, knit and embroidered things, fringed things. "Did by the inmates," says she, proud. That word "inmates" is to the word "people" what the word "support" is to the word "share." It's a word we could spare.

I looked at the things in the case—hours and hours and hours the fingers of the women upstairs had worked on 'em—intricate counting, difficult stitches, pretty patterns. And each of them was marked with a price tag. The County House inmates had got 'em hung out there in the hope of earning a little money. One was a bed-spread—a whole crocheted bed-spread. And one—one was a dress crocheted from collar to hem, and hung on with all sorts of crazy crocheted ends and tassels so—I knew—to make the job last a little longer. And when I saw that, I grabbed the tall, thick matron by the arm and I shook her a little.

"What was we doing," I says, "that these folks wasn't taught to do some kind of work so's they could have kept out of the poor house?"

She looked at me odd and cool.

"Why," she said, "my dear Miss Marsh, it's being in here that gives 'em the leisure to make the things at all!"

What was the use of talking to her? And besides being unreasonable, she was one of them that you're awful put to it to keep from being able not to right down dislike. And I went along the passage thinking: "She acts like the way things are is the way things ought to be. But it always seems to me that the way things ought to be is the best way things could be. For the earth ain't so full of the fulness thereof but that we could all do something to make it a little more so."

And then the thing happened that opened the door to all I'd been thinking about, and let me slip through inside.

Being I was there, I dropped in a minute to see old Grandma Stuart. She was one of the eighty "inmates." Up in the ward where she was sitting, there were twenty beds. And between each two beds was a shelf and a washbasin, and over it a hook. And old Grandma Stuart sat there by her bed and her shelf and her hook. She was old and white, and she had fine wrinkles, like a dead flower. She drew me down to her, with her cold hands.

"Miss Marsh," she said, "I got two-three things."

"Yes," I says, "well, that's nice," I says. And wondered if that was the right thing to say to her.

"But I ain't got any box," she says. "They keep the things and bring 'em to us clean every time. And I ain't got any box."

"That's so, you ain't," says I, looking at her shelf.

"I put my things in my dress," she says, "but they always fall out. And I've got to stop to pick 'em up. And *she* don't like it."

No. The matron wouldn't like it. I knew that. She was one of them that the thing was the thing even if it was something else.

"And so I thought," says Grandma Stuart, "that if I had a pocket, I could put my things in that. I thought they wouldn't fall out if I had a pocket. *She* says she can't be making pockets for every one. But I keep thinking if I had a pocket.... It's these things I've got," she says.

She took from her dress three things: A man's knife, a child's ring, and a door-key.

"It was the extry key to my house," she said. "I—brought it along. And I thought if I had a pocket...."

...I sat there with her till the lights come out. I promised to come next day and bring her a little calico pocket. And then I set and let her talk to me—about how things use' to be. When at last the matron come to take 'em away to be fed, I went out, and I ran down the road in the dark. And it was one of the times when the world of life is right close up, and you can all but touch it, and you can almost hear what it says, and you know that it can hear you—yes, and you almost know that it's waiting, eager, to hear what *you* are going to say to it. For one force breathes through things, trying to let us know it's there. It was speaking to me through that wrecked home of Grandma Stuart's—through the man's knife, the child's ring, the door-key; and through the pitiful, clever, crocheted stuff in the glass case in the County House; and through David, and through all them that we were trying to fix up a club for—like a pleasant plaster for something that couldn't be touched by the remedy.

Out there in the soft night, the world looked different. I donno if you'll know what I mean, but it was like the world I knew had suddenly slipped inside another world—like a shell; and the other one was bigger and better and cut in a pattern that we haven't grown to—yet. In the west a little new moon was showing inside the gold circle of the big coming full moon. And it seemed to me as if the world that I was in must be just the little thin promise of the world that could be—if we knew. Sometimes we do know. Sometimes, for just a minute, we see it. That night was a night when I know that I saw. After you see, you never forget.

"Life is something else than what we think it is," I says to myself as I ran along the road in the dark. "It's something better than we think it is."

As I ran, I stopped in to Mis' Beach's house and asked for something. "Oh, Mis' Beach," I says, "Oh, David! Will you let me take something? Will you let me borrow the clock you put together without anybody telling you how? Just for this evening?"

They said they would and they didn't question that, particular, either. And I took the clock. And being David was going for the yeast, he came out with me, and we went on together. He ran beside me, the little lad, with his hand in mine. And as I ran, it seemed to me that I wasn't Calliope Marsh any more, but that I was the immemorial woman, running with the immemorial child, toward the hope of the better thing, always the better thing.

Past the Post-Office Hall I went, already lighted for the Business Meeting, and on to Abigail Arnold's Home Bakery.

Abigail was sitting, dressed and ready, with her list in her hand. But when she saw me she burst out with some strange excitement in her face:

"Calliope!" she says. "Silas has been here. He said you hadn't handed in your report. I—I don't think he expects you to go to the meeting. I know he didn't expect me."

"Didn't he now?" I says. "Very well then, he didn't. Are you ready?"

"But, Calliope——" says she.

"Are you a business woman in this town, or are you not?" I asked her.

Abigail has had her Bakery for twenty years now, and has paid off its mortgage that her husband bequeathed her.

"Come," says I. And she did.

We went down the street to the Post-Office store building, all lighted up. We went up the stairs, and slipped into some seats by the door. I don't think Silas, the chairman, see us come in. He can't of, because he failed to explode. He just kept on conducting the meeting called to consider the future prosperity of Friendship Village and balancing on his toes.

While they talked, I set there, looking at them. Sixty men or so they were—the men that had made Friendship Village. Yes, such as it was, these men had made it. It was Silas that had built up his business and added to it, till he employed forty-two folks. Timothy Toplady had done the same and had encouraged three-four others to come in to open up new things for the town. It was Timothy stood back of Zittelhof when he added furniture to his undertaking business, and that started the agitation for the cheese factory out in the hills, and that got the whole county excited about having good roads. And it was these men and Eppleby Holcomb and some others that had got the new bridge and the water works and more than these. And while I set there looking at them, it come flooding over me the skill and the energy and the patience and the dogged hard work that it had meant for them sixty men to get us where we were, and from my heart I was thankful to 'em. And then I put my mind on what they were a-saying:

"An up-to-date, hustling little town," I kept hearing. "The newer business methods." "Good openings." "Opportunities for hustlers." "Need of live wires." "Encourage industry." "Advance the town, advance the town, advance the town." And the thoughts that had been formed in no account clots in my head suddenly took shape in one thought, with the whole of day-light turned on to it.

So, as quick as the business part seemed to me to be done, I rose up and told Silas we had our reports to make, Abigail and me, about the Evening Club.

"Well," says Silas, "this whole thing is being done irregular. Most irregular. But you go on ahead, and we'll be glad to listen if you think you have anything to say, bearing on to—er—what we're up to."

And that was all right, and I took it so, because it was meant right.

I donno what there was to be afraid of. All of those men we'd known for years. We'd worked with 'em shoulder to shoulder in church affairs. We'd stood equal to 'em in school affairs, and often agreed with 'em. We'd even repeatedly paid one of 'em our taxes. And yet because it was a Business Men's meeting, we felt kind of abashed or askant or something, Abigail and me.

Abigail reported first, about the thirty odd she'd been to see. "But," she winds up, "Calliope's got something to say that I agree to, over and above the report. We've talked it over, her and me, and—" she adds with her nice dignity, "as a Friendship Village business woman, I'm going to leave her speak for me."

So I said what I had to say about them I'd been to see, and what they had said about the club. And then I come to the heart of it, and I held up David's little clock. I told 'em about it, and about him. I suppose everybody else has stories to tell like David's, about the folks, young or old, that is living graves, little or big, of the kind of skill and energy and patience that they've never had the chance or the courage or the little will-power inside 'em—to develop. And there it stays in 'em, undeveloped, till they die. I believe it's truer of all of us—of you and me—than we've any idea of. And this is what I tried to say to 'em that night, when I showed 'em David's little clock. I didn't say anything about the girls to Mis' Cripps's boarding house—I kept them, and the rest of 'em, in my heart, along with that crocheted dress up to the County House, and Grandma Stuart's wreck of a home—the man's knife, the child's ring, the door-key. And I says:

"Now, we've visited all these folks that the Evening Club was thought of for. And we've found most of 'em in favor of having the club. I'm free to confess that I hoped some of 'em wouldn't be. I hoped some of 'em would say they'd rather be paid better wages than to be give a club. But perhaps it's all right. Mebbe the club is one step more we've got to take before we can get down to the big thing underneath it all. But it ain't the last step—and I'd almost rather not bother with it—I'd almost rather get on to the big thing right away."

"May I ask," snaps out Silas, clean forgetting his chairmanshipping and acting like he was talking to me in the Post-Office store beside the cheese, "may I ask what you mean by the 'big thing'?"

"Oh," I says, "that's what I've been thinking about while I set here. Oh," I says, "you men—you've made the town. You've done everything once. Do it again—now when the next thing is here to do. You've done your best with your own property and your own homes. Now do your best with folks!"

"Ain't that the purpose of this here club we're a-talking about?" says Silas. "Ain't that what I been a-saying? What do you mean—folks?" Silas winds up, irritable. Silas knows customers, agents, correspondents, partners, clients, colleagues, opponents, plaintiffs, defendants *and* competitors. But he don't know *folks*.

"Folks," I says. "Why, folks, Silas. Why, here in this room with you that we say have made Friendship Village, are setting them sixty-one employees of yours that have helped make it too. And all the tens that will come afterward, and that have come before to help to make the village by the work of their hands. They belong—they're the village. They're us. Oh, let's not do things *for* them—let's do things *with* them. Let's meet all together, employers and employees, men and women, and let's take up together the job of being a town. Let's not any of us have more than our share, and then deal out little clubs, and old furniture, and magazines, and games to the rest of us. You men are finding out that all your old catch words about advancing the town and making business opportunities, have got something lacking in them, after all. And us women are beginning to see that twenty houses to a block, each keeping clean and orderly and planted on its own hook, each handing out old clothes and toys down to the Flats, each living its own life of cleanliness and home and victual-giving-at-Christmas, that that ain't being a town after all. It isn't enough. Oh, deep inside us all ain't there something that says, I ain't you, nor you, nor you, nor five thousand of you. I'm all of you. I'm one. 'When,' it says, 'are you going to understand, that not till I can act like one, one united one, can I give any glimpse whatever of what people might be?' Don't let's us go on advancing business and multiplying our little clubs and philanthropies. Instead, let's get together—in the kind of meetings they use' to have in the old first days in America—and let's just talk over the next step in what's to become of us. Let's dream—real far. Let's dream farther than gift-giving—and on up to wages—and mebbe a good deal farther than that. Let's dream the farthest that folks could go...."

I didn't know but they'd think I was crazy. But I'd be glad to be that kind of crazy. And the glory is that more folks and more folks are getting crazy the same way.

But they didn't think so—I know they didn't. Because when I got through, they clapped their hands, hard and hearty—all but Silas, that don't think a chairman had ought to show any pleased emotion. And times now when I'm lonesome, I like to remember the rest of the talk, and it warms my heart to remember it, and I like to think about it.

For we give up having the club. Nobody said much of anything more about it, after we got Silas silenced. And this was the notice we put the next night in the Friendship *Evening Daily*. Nobody knows better than I the long road that there is to travel before we can really do what we dreamed out a little bit about. Nobody better than I knows how slow it is going to be. But

I tell you, it is going to be. And the notice we put in the paper was the first little step we took. And I believe that notice holds the heart of to-day.

It said:

"Will all them that's interested in seeing Friendship Village made as much a town as it could be, for all of us and for the children of all of us, meet together in Post-Office Hall to-morrow night, at 7 o'clock, to talk over if we're doing it as good as we could."

For there was business. And then there was big business. But the biggest business is taking employers and employees, and all men and women—yes, and inmates too—and turning them into folks.

THE PRODIGAL GUEST

Aunt Ellis wrote to me:

"Dear Calliope: Now come and pay me the visit. You've never been here since the time I had sciatica and was cross. Come now, and I'll try to hold my temper and my tongue."

I wrote back to her:

"I'll come. I was saving up to buy a new cook-stove next fall, but I'll bring my cook-stove and come in time for the parade. I did want to see that."

She answered:

"Mercy, Calliope, I might have known it! You always did love a circus in the village, and these women are certainly making a circus parade of themselves. However, we'll even drive down to see them do it, if you'll really come. Now you know how much I want you."

"I might have known," I said to myself, "that Aunt Ellis would be like that. The poor thing has had such an easy time that she can't help it. She thinks what's been, is."

She wrote me that she was coming in from the country an hour after my train got there, but that the automobile would be there for me. And I wrote her that I would come down the platform with my umbrella up, so's her man would know me; and so I done, and he picked me out real ready.

When we got to her big house, that somehow looked so used to being a big house, there was a little boy sitting on the bottom step, half asleep, with a big box.

"What's the matter, lamb?" I says.

"Beg pad', ma'am, he's likely waitin' to beg," says the chauf—— that word. "I'd go right by if I was you."

But the little fellow'd woke up and looked up.

"I can't find the place," he says, and stuck out his big box. The man looked at the label. "They ain't no such number in this street," says he. "It's a mistake."

The little fellow kind of begun to cry, and the wind was blowing up real bitter. I made out that him and his family made toys for the uptown shops, and somebody in our neighborhood had ordered some direct, and he was afraid to go home without the money. I didn't have any money to give him, but I says to the chauf——

"Ask him where he lives, will you? And see if we'd have time to take him home before Mis' Winthrop's train gets in."

The chauf—— done it, some like a prime minister, and he says, cold, he thought we'd have time, and I put the baby in the car. He was a real sweet little fellow, about seven. He told me his part in making the toys, and his mother's, and his two little sisters', and I give him the rest o' my lunch, and he knew how to laugh when he got the chance, and we had a real happy time of it. And we come to his home.

Never, not if I live till after my dying day, will I forget the looks of that back upstairs place he called home, nor the smell of it—the smell of it. The waxy woman that was his mother, in a red waist, and with a big weight of hair, had forgot how to look surprised—that struck me as so awful—she'd forgot how to look surprised, just the same as a grand lady that's learned not to; and there was the stumpy man that grunted for short instead of bothering with words; and the two little girls that might of been anybody's—if they'd been clean—one of 'em with regular portrait hair. I stayed a minute, and give 'em the cost of about one griddle of my cook-stove, and then I went to the station to meet Aunt Ellis. And I poured it all out to her, as soon as she'd give me her cheek to kiss.

"So you haven't had any tea!" she said, getting in the automobile. "I'm sorry you've been so annoyed the first thing."

"Annoyed!" I says over. "Annoyed! Well, yes," I says, "poor people is real annoying. I wonder we have 'em."

I was dying to ask her about the parade, but I didn't like to; till after we'd had dinner in front of snow and silver and sparkles and so on, and had gone in her parlor-with-another-name, and set down in the midst of flowers and shades and lace, and rugs the color of different kinds of preserves, and wood-work like the skin of a cooked prune. Then I says:

"You know I'm just dying to hear about the parade."

She lifted her hand and shut her eyes, brief.

"Calliope," she says, "I don't know what has come over women. They seem to want to attract attention to themselves. They seem to want to be conspicuous and talked about. They seem to want——"

"They want lots o' things," says I, dry, "but it ain't any of them, Aunt Ellis. What time does the parade start?"

"You're bound to see it?" she says. "When I think of my dear Miss Markham—they used to say her school taught not manners, but manner—and what she would say to the womanhood of to-day.... We'll drive down if you say so, Calliope—but I don't know whether I can bear it long."

"Manner," I says over. "Manner. That's just what we're trying to learn now, manner of being alive. We haven't known very much about that, it seems."

I kept thinking that over next day when we were drawn up beside the curb in the car, waiting for them to come. "We're trying to learn manner at last—the manner of being alive." There were lots of other cars, with women so pretty you felt like crying up into the sky to ask there if we knew for sure what all that perfection was for, or if there was something else to it we didn't know—yet. And thousands of women on foot, and thousands of women in windows.... I looked at them and wondered if they thought we were, and life was, as decent as we and it could be, and, if not, how they were preparing to help change it. I thought of the rest that were up town in colored nests, and them that were down town in factories, and them that were to home in the villages, and them that were out all along the miles and miles to the other ocean, just the same way. And here was going to come this little line of women walking along the street, a little line of women that thought they see new life for us all, and see it more abundant.

"Manner," I says, "we're just beginning to learn manner."

Then, way down the avenue, they began to come. By ones and by fours and by eights, with colors and with music and with that that was greater than all of them—the tramp and tramp of feet; feet that weren't dancing to balls, nor racking up and down in shops buying pretty things to make 'em power, nor just paddling around a kitchen the same as mine had always done—but feet that were marching, in a big, peaceful army, towards the place where the big, new tasks of to-morrow are going to be, that won't interfere with the best tasks of yesterday no more than the earth's orbit interferes with its whirling round and round.

"That's it," I says, "that's it! We've been whirling round and round, manufacturing the days and the nights, and we never knew we had an orbit too."

So they come, till they begun to pass where we were—some heads up, some eyes down, women, women, marching to a tune that was being beat out by thousands of hearts all over the world. I'd never seen women like this before. I saw them like I'd never seen them—I felt I was one of 'em like I'd never known that either. And I saw what they saw and I felt what they felt more than I ever knew I done.

Then I heard Aunt Ellis making a little noise in her breath.

"The bad taste of it—the bad taste of it, Calliope!" she said. "When I was a girl we used to use the word ladylike—we used to strive to deserve it. It's a beautiful word. But these——"

"We've been ladylike," says I, sad, "for five or ten thousand years, and where has it got us to?"

"Oh, but, Calliope, they like it—they like the publicity and the notoriety and the——"

I kept still, but I hurt all over me. I can stand anything only hearing that they like it—the way Aunt Ellis meant. I thought to myself that I bet the folks that used to watch martyrs were heard to say that martyrs prob'ly thought flames was becoming or they wouldn't be burnt. But when I looked at Aunt Ellis sitting in her car with her hand over her eyes, it come over me all at once the tragedy of it—of all them that watch us cast their old ideals in new forms—their old ideals.

All of a sudden I stood up in the car. The parade had got blocked for a minute, and right in front of the curb where we stood I saw a woman I knew; a little waxy-looking thing, that couldn't look surprised or exalted or afraid or anything else, and I knew her in a minute—even to the red calico waist and the big weight of hair, just as I had seen her by the toy table in her "home" the night before. And there she was, marching. And here was Aunt Ellis and me.

I leaned over and touched Aunt Ellis.

"You mustn't mind," I says; "I'm going too."

She looked at me like I'd turned into somebody else.

"I'm going out there," I says, "with them. I see it like they do—I feel it like they do. And them that sees it and feels it and don't help it along is holding it back. I'll find my way home...."

I ran to them. I stepped right out in the street among them and fell in step with them, and then I saw something. While I was making my way through the crowd to them the line had passed on, and them I was with was all in caps and gowns. I stopped still in the road.

"Great land!" I says to the woman nearest, "you're college, ain't you? And I never even got through high school."

She smiled and put out her hand.

"Come on," she says.

Whatever happens to me afterward, I've had that hour. No woman that has ever had it will ever forget it—the fear and the courage, the pride and the dread, the hurt and the power and the glory. I don't know whether it's the way—but what is the way? I only know that all down the street, between the rows of watching faces, I could think of that little waxy woman going along ahead, and of the kind of place that she called home, and of the kind of a life she and her children had. And I knew then and I know now that the poverty and the dirt and some of the death in the world is our job, it's our job too. And if they won't let us do it ladylike, we'll do it just plain.

When I got home, Aunt Ellis was having tea. She smiled at me kind of sad, as a prodigal guest deserved.

"Aunt Ellis," I says, "I've give 'em the rest of my cook-stove money, except my fare home."

"My poor Calliope," she says, "that's just the trouble. You all go to such hysterical extremes."

I'd heard that word several times on the street. I couldn't stand it any longer.

"Was that hysterics to-day?" I says. "I've often wondered what they're like. I've never had the time to have them, myself. Well," I says, tired but serene, "if that was hysterics, leave 'em make the most of it."

I looked at her, meditative.

"Miss Markham and you and the women that marched to-day and me," I says. "And a hundred years from now we'll all be conservatives together. And there'll be some big new day coming on that would startle me now, just the same as it would you. But the way I feel to-night, honest—I donno but I'm ready for that one too."

MR. DOMBLEDON

He came to my house one afternoon when I was just starting off to get a-hold of two cakes for the next meeting of the Go-lightly club, and my mind was all trained to a peak, capped with the cakes.

Says he: "Have you got rooms to let?"

For a minute I didn't answer him, I was so knee deep in looking at the little boy he had with him—the cutest, lovin'est little thing I'd ever seen. But though I love the human race and admire to see it took care of, I couldn't sense my way clear to taking a boy into my house. Boys belongs to the human race, to be sure, just as whirling egg-beaters belongs to omelettes, but much as I set store by omelettes I couldn't invite a whirling egg-beater into my home permanent.

Says I: "Not to boys."

He laughed—kind of a pleasant laugh, fringed all round with little laughs.

"Oh," he says, "we ain't boys."

"Well," says I, "one of you is. And I don't ever rent to 'em. They ain't got enough silence to 'em," I says, as delicate as I could.

Just then the little lad himself looked up innocent and took a hand without meaning to.

"Is your doggy home?" says he.

"Yes," I says, "curled up on the back mat." I felt kind of glad I didn't have to tell him I didn't have one.

"I'd like," says he, grave, "to *fluffle* it till you're through."

"So do," says I, hearty, and he trotted round the house like a little minister.

I kind o' tiptoed after him, casual. All of a sudden I wanted to see what he done. His father come behind me on the boards, and we saw the little fellow bend over and pat Mac, my water spaniel, as gentle as if he'd been cut glass. The little boy looked awful cute, bending over, his short hair sticking out at the back. I can see him yet.

"How much," says I, "would you want to pay for your room?"

"Well," says his father, "not much. But I give a guess your price is what it's worth—no more, no less."

I hadn't paid much attention to him before that, but I see now he was a wonderful, nice-spoken little man, with the kind of eyes that look like the sitting-room—and not like the parlor. I can't bear parlor eyes.

"Come and look at the room," says I, and rented it to him out of hand. And Mr. Dombledon—his name was—and Donnie—that was the little fellow—went off for their baggage, and I went off for my cakes; and what they was reflecting on I donno, but my own reflect was that it's a wise minute can tell what the next one is going to pop open and let out. But I like it that way. I'm a natural-born vaudevillian. I love to see what's coming next.

Well, the next thing was, after I got my two club cakes both provided for, that it turned out Mr. Dombledon was an agent, selling "notions, knick-knacks and anything o' that," he told me; and he use' to start out at seven o'clock in the morning, with his satchel in one hand and his little boy, more or less, in the other.

"Land," says I to him after a few days, "don't your little boy get wore to the bone tramping around with you like that?"

"Some," says he; "but I carry him part of the way."

"Carry him?" says I, "and tote that heavy knick-knack notion satchel?"

"Well," says he, "I don't mind it. What I'm always thinking is this: What if I didn't have him to tote."

"True enough," says I, and couldn't say another word.

But of course the upstart and offshoot of that was that before the week was out, I'd invited Mr. Dombledon to leave the little fellow with me, some days, while he went off. And he done so, grateful, but making a curious provision.

"It'd be grand for him," says he; "they's only just one thing: Would—would you promise not to leave him hear anybody say anything anyways cross?"

"Well," says I, judicious, "I donno's I'm what-you-might-say cross. Not systematic. But—I might be a little crispy."

"I ain't afraid o' you," says he, real flattering. "But don't leave him hear anybody—well, snap anybody up."

"All right," says I, "I won't. I like," I says, "to get out o' the way of that myself."

"Well, and then," he says, "I guess you'll think I'm real particular. But—would you promise not to leave him go outside the yard?"

"Sure," says I, "only when I'm with him."

"I guess you'll think I'm real particular," he says again, in his kind of gentle voice without any sizin' to it, "but I mean not even then. Days when you're goin' out, I'll take him with me."

"Sure," says I, wondering all over me, but not letting on all I wondered, like you can't in society. And I actually looked forward to having the little thing around the house with me, me that has always been down on mice, moths, bats and boys.

The next thing was, Would he stay with me? And looking to this end I contrived, some skillful, to be baking cookies the first morning his pa went off. Mis' Puppy had happened in early to get some blueing, and she was sitting at one end of my cook table when Donnie came trotting out with his father, that always preferred the back door. ("It feels more like I lived here," says he, wishful, "if you let me come in the back door." And I was the last one to deny him that. Once when I went visiting, I got so homesick to go in the back door that it was half my reason for leaving 'em.)

"Now then," I says to the little fellow that morning, "you just set here with us and see me make cookies. I'll cut you out a soldier cooky," says I.

"Wiv *buttins?*" he asks, and climbed up on his knees on a chair by the table and let his father go off without him, nice as the nicest. "I likes 'em wiv buttins," he says—and Mis' Puppy sort of kindled up in her throat, like a laugh that wants to love somebody.

I donno as I know how to say it, but he was the kind of a little chap that, when you're young, you always think *your* little chap is going to be. Then when they do come, sometimes they're dear and all that, but they ain't quite exactly the way you thought of them being—though you forget that they ain't, and you forget everything but loving 'em. But it was like this little boy was the way you'd meant. It wasn't so much the way he looked—though he was beautiful, beautiful like some of the things you think and not like a calendar—but it was the way he *was*, kind of close up to you, and his breath coming past, and something you couldn't name gentling round him. His father hadn't been gone ten minutes when the little thing let me kiss him.

" 'At was my last one," he explained, sort of sorry, to Mis' Puppy. "But you can have a bite off my soldier. That's a better kiss."

Mis' Puppy watched him for a while—he was sitting close down by the oven door to hear his soldier say *Hurrah* the minute he was baked, if you please—and she kind of moved like her thoughts scraped by each other, and she says—and spells one word of it out:

"Where do you s'pose his m-o-t-h-e-r is?"

"My land, d-e-d," I answers, "or she'd be setting over there kissing the back of his neck in the hollow."

"I've got," says Mis' Puppy, "kind of an idea she ain't. Your boarder," she says, "don't look to me real what you might call a widower. He ain't the air of one that's had things ciphered out for him," says she. "It's more like he was still a-browsing round the back o' the book for the answer."

And that was true, when you come to think of it; he did seem sort of quick-moved and hopeful, more like when you sit down to the table than when you shove back.

I told Mis' Puppy, private, what his father had said to me about his not hearing anything spoke cross; and she nodded, like it was something she'd got all thought out, with tags on.

"I was a-wondering the other day," she says, dreamy, "what I'd of been like if nobody had ever yipped out at me. I s'pose none of us knows."

"Likewise," says I, "what we'd be like if we'd never yipped out to no one else."

"That's so," she says, "ain't it? The two fits together like a covered bake-dish."

"Ain't you 'fraid he'll shoot the oven door down if you don't let him out pitty quick?" says Donnie, trying to see how near he could get his ear to the crack to hear that "Hurrah."

Four days the little boy done that, stayed with me as contented as a kitten while his father went agenting; and then the fifth day he had to take him with him, because there come on what I'd been getting the cakes for—the quarterly meeting of the Go-lightly club.

The Go-lightly club is sixteen Red Barns ladies—and me—that's all passed the sixty-year-old mark, and has had to begin to go lightly. We picked the name as being so literal, grievous-true as to our powers and, same time, airy and happy sounding, just like we hope we'll be clear up to the last of the last of us. We had a funny motto and, those days, it use' to be a secret. We'd lit on it when we was first deciding to have the club.

"What do we *want* a club for anyhow?" old Mis' Lockmeyer had said, that don't really enjoy anything that she ain't kicked out at first.

"Why," says little Mis' Pettibone, kind of gentle and final, "just to kind of make life nice."

"Well," says Mis' Lockmeyer, "we got to go awful light on it, our age."

And we put both them principles into our constitution:

"Name: The name of this club shall be the Go-lightly club, account of the character of its members.

"Object: The object of this club shall be to make life nice.

"No officers. No dues. No real regular meetings.

"Picnic supper when any."

And Mis' Wilme had insisted on adding:

"Every-day clothes or not so much so."

Our next meeting was going to be at Mis' Elkhorn's that lives out of town about two miles along the old Tote road, and we was looking forward to it considerable. We'd put it off several times; one week the ice-cream sociable was going to be, and one week the circus was to the next town, and so on—we never like to interfere with any other social going-ons.

None of us having a horse, we hired the rig—that's the three-seat canopy-top from the livery—and was all drove out together by Jem Meddledipper. And it was real nice and festive, with our lunch baskets all piled up in the back and, as Mis' Wilme put it: "Nothing to do till time to set the pan-cakes." And when we got outside the City limits—we're just a village, but we've got 'em marked "City Limits," because that always seems the name of 'em—Mis' Pettibone, that's a regular one for entering into things—you know some just is and some just ain't and the two never change places on no occasion whatever—she kind of pitched in and sung in her nice little voice that she calls her sopralto, because it ain't placed much of any place. She happened on a church piece—I donno if you know it?—the one that's got a chorus that goes first

"Loving-kindness"

all wavy, like a little stream trickling along; and then another part chimes in,

"Loving-kindness"

all wavy, like another little stream trickling along, and then everybody clamps down on

"Loving-kindness—oh, how great!"

like the whole nice sweep of the river? Well, that was the one she sung. And being it's a terrible catchy tune, and most of us was brought up on it and has been haunted by it for days together from bed to bed, we all more or less joined in with what little vocal pans we had, and we sung it off and on all the way out.

We was singing it, I recollect, when we come in sight of the Toll Gate House. The Toll Gate House has been there for years, ever since the Tote road got made into a real road, and then it got paid for, and the toll part stopped; and now the City rents the house—there's a place we always say "City" again—to most anybody, usually somebody poor, with a few chickens and takes in washings and ain't much of any other claim to being thought of, as claims seem to go.

"Who lives in the Toll Gate House now, I wonder?" says Mis' Pettibone, breaking off her song.

"Land, nobody," says Mis' Lockmeyer; "it's all fell in on itself—my land," she says, "the door's open. Let's stop and report 'em, so be it's been tramps."

So we made Jem Meddledipper stop, and somebody was just going to get out when a woman come to the door.

She was a little woman, with kind of a pindling expression, looking as if she'd started in good and strong, but life had kind of shaved her down till there wasn't as much left of her, strictly speaking, as'd make a regular person. A person, but not one that looks well and happy the way "person" means to you, when you say the word. She had on a what-had-been navy-blue what-had-been alpaca, but both them attributes had got wore down past the nap. A little girl was standing close beside her—a nice little thing, with her hair sticking up on top like a candle-flame, and tied with a string.

"My land," says Mis' Lockmeyer right out, "are you livin' *here*?" Mis' Lockmeyer is like that—she always wears her face inside-out with all the expression showing.

But the woman wasn't hurt. She smiled a little, and when she smiled I thought she looked real sweet.

"Yes," she said, "I am. It—it don't look real like it, does it?"

"Well," puts in Mis' Pettibone, "gettin' settled so——"

"Oh," says the woman, "I been here a month."

And Mis' Lockmeyer, wishing to make amends and pull her foot out, planted the other right along side of it instead.

"Do you sell anything? Or sew anything? Or wash and iron anything?" she asks.

And the woman says: "I sew and wash and iron anything I can do home, with my little girl. But I ain't a thing in the world to sell."

"Of course you ain't," says Mis' Lockmeyer soothing, and hoping to make it better still.

"Well," says Mis' Puppy hearty, "I tell you what. We'll be out to see you in a little bit, if you want us to."

My land, the woman's face—I donno whether you've ever seen anybody's face lit up from the inside with the light fair showing through all the pores like little windows? Hers done it. She didn't say nothing—she just done that. And we drove on.

"Land," says Mis' Pettibone, thoughtful, "how like each other folks are, no matter how not-like they seem to the folks you think they ain't one bit like."

"Ain't they—ain't they?" says I, hearty. And I guess we all felt the same.

Nobody was absent to the club that afternoon, but Mis' Elkhorn's sitting-room was big enough so's we could get in. None of us could bear a parlor club meeting. Our ideas always set in our heads to a parlor-meeting, called to order by rapping on something. But here at Mis' Elkhorn's we were out in the sitting-room, with the red table-spread on and the plants growing and the spice-cake smelling through the kitchen door. And you'd think things would of gone as smooth as glass.

Instead of which, I donno what on earth ailed us. But when we got to sitting down, sewing, it was like some kind of little fine dislocation had took place in the air.

Mis' Puppy had brought a centre-piece to work on, big as a rug, all drawn work and hemstitching and embroidery. And somehow Mis' Pettibone, that only embroiders useful, couldn't stand it.

"My, Mis' Puppy," she says, "I shouldn't think you could get a bit of house-work done, making that so lavish."

Mis' Puppy shut her lips so tight it jerked her head.

"I don't scrub out continual, same as some," she says.

"If you mean me," says Mis' Pettibone, tart, "I guess I can do housework as easy as the most."

"I heard there's those that can—where it don't show," says Mis' Puppy, some goaded beyond what she meant.

"Mean to say?" snaps Mis' Pettibone.

"Oh, nothin'," says Mis' Puppy, "only to them that their backs the coat fits."

"I never was called shiftless since I was born a wife and a housekeeper," says Mis' Pettibone, bordering on tearful.

"Oh, *was* you born a house-keeper, Mis' Pettibone?" says Mis' Puppy, sweet.

Then Mis' Pettibone went in and set on the foot of the bed where we'd laid our things, and cried; and one or two of us went in and sort o' poored her.

And, land, when we'd got her to come out, the first thing we heard was Mis' Lockmeyer pitching into Mis' Wilme.

"Anybody that can say I don't make ice-cream as cheap as the best ain't any of an ice-cream judge," she was saying hot, "be they you or be they better."

"I wasn't saying a word about *cheap*," says Mis' Wilme, "I was talking about *good*."

"Well," says Mis' Lockmeyer, "I thought I made it good."

"Not with the little dab of cream you was just mentioning, you can't," says Mis' Wilme, firm. "It ain't reasonable *nor* chemical."

"Don't you think your long words is goin' to impress me," says Mis' Lockmeyer, more and more het up.

"Well, ladies," says Mis' Elkhorn, humorous, "nobody can make it any colder'n anybody else, anyhow."

Somebody pitched in then, hasty and peaceful, and went to talking about Cemetery; and it looked like we was launched on a real quiet subject.

"I guess we've all got more friends up there then we've got in town," says I. "When we go up there to walk on Sundays, I declare if I had to bow to all the graves I recognize I'd be kep' busy."

"I know," says Mis' Wilme, "when my niece was here from the City she said she had eighty on her calling list. 'Well,' I says, 'I've got that many if I count the graves I know.'"

"Most of my acquaintances," says Mis' Lockmeyer, sighing, "is in their coffins. I says to my husband when I looked over the *Daily* the other night: That most of the Local Items and Supper Table Jottings for me now would have to be dated Cemetery Lot."

"I know, ladies," says Mis' Puppy, dreamy, "but ain't it real aristocratic to live in a place so long that you know all the graves. We ain't got much else to be aristocratic about. But that's real like them county families you read about," she says.

And up flared Mis' Pettibone. "I donno's there's any need to make it so pointed to us that ain't lived here so very long," she said, "and that ain't any friends at all in your Cemetery."

"Oh, well," says Mis' Puppy, indulgent, "of course there's them distinctions in any town."

I was just feeling thankful from my bones out that they hadn't met to my house, with Donnie staying home, when Mis' Elkhorn come in from the kitchen to tell us supper was ready. And when she opened the door the smell of hot waffles come a dilly-nipping in, and it made me feel so kind of cozy and busy and alive and glad that I burst right out:

"Shucks, ladies!" I says. "So be we peck around for 'em I bet we could find things to fuss over right till the hearse backs up to the door."

They all laughed a little then, but that was part from feeling embarrassed at going out to supper, like you always are. And when we did get out there, everybody scrabbled around to get away from whoever had just been her enemy. We didn't say much while we et—like you don't in company; and I set there thinking:

"The Go-lightly club. The Go-lightly club. To make life nice." And I thought how we'd sung that song of ours all the way out. And I made up my mind that, after supper, when they was feeling limber from food, I'd try to say something about it.

But I didn't. I just got started on it—introduced by telling 'em some nice little things about Donnie's sayings and doings to my house, when Mis' Lockmeyer broke in, sympathetic.

"Ain't he a great care?" says she.

"Yes," says I, "he is. And so is everything on top of this earth that's worth having. Life thrown in."

And then I see they was all rustling to go home—giving reasons of clothes to sprinkle or bread to set or grandchild to put to bed or plants to cover up. So I kep' still, and mogged along home with 'em. But I did say to Mis' Pettibone on the back seat:

"We better quit off club. If we can't meet folks without laying awake nights over the things that's been said to us, we better never meet. 'To make life nice,' " says I. "Ain't club a travnasty, or whatever that word is?"

"I know it," she says awful sober, and I see she was grieving some too. And we was all pretty still, going home. So still that we could all hear Jem Meddledipper, that had caught the run o' that tune from us in the afternoon and was driving us home by it, and the wheels went round to it—

"Lovin'-kindness ... lovin'-kindness ... lovin'-kindness,
oh, how great,"

—and it was sung considerable better than any of us had sung it.

But anyway, the result of leaving early was that we got to the Toll Gate House before dark, and I'll never forget the thing we saw. Standing in the door of the little house was the woman we'd spoke with in the afternoon, and she was wearing the same ex-blue alpaca. But now she'd been and got out from somewheres and put on a white straw hat, with little pink roses all around it. And like lightning I sensed that she'd watched for us to come back and had gone and got the hat out and put it on, so's to let us know she had that one decent thing to wear.

"Jem," I says, "stop."

I donno rightly why, but I clambered down out of the rig, and I says to the woman: "Let me come in a minute—can I? I want to talk to you about—about some sewing," says I, that's sewed every rag I've had on my back most ever since I was clothed in any. But all of a sudden, her getting out that hat made me feel I just had to get up close to her, like you will.

But when I stepped inside, I forgot all about the sewing.

"My land, my dear," I says, or it might have been, "My dear, my land," I was that taken-back and upset, "you'd ought to have this ceiling mended."

For the plaster had fell off full half of it and the roof leaked; and there wasn't very much of any furniture, to clap the climax.

"The City won't do anything," says she. "They're going to tear it down. And the rent ain't much—so I want to stay."

"Well," says I, "I'm going to bring you out some napkins to hem next week—can I?"—me having bought new before then so's to have some work for Missionary Society, so why not now? And her face lit up that same way from inside.

When I'd got back in the rig, and we'd drove a little way by, I spoke to the rest about her going and putting on the hat. Some of 'em had sensed it, and some of 'em hadn't—like some will and some won't sense every created thing. And when we all did get a-hold of it—well, I can't hardly tell you what it done. But there was something there in the rig with us that hadn't been there before, and that come with a rush now, and that done a thing to us all alike. I can't rightly say what it was, or what it done; but I guess Mis' Puppy come as near it as anybody:

"Oh, ladies," she says, kind of hushed, "don't that seem like—well, don't it make you feel—well, I donno, but ain't it just...."

She kind of petered off, and it was Mis' Pettibone, her enemy, that answered.

"Don't it, Mis' Puppy?" she says, "*Don't* it?" And we all felt the same way. Or similar. And we never said a word, but we told each other good night, I noticed, about three times apiece, all around. And out of the fulness of the lump in my throat, I says:

"Ladies! I invite the Go-lightly club to meet with me to-morrow afternoon. Don't bring anything but sandwiches and your plates and spoons. I'll open the sauce and make the tea and whip up some drop sponge cakes. And meantime, let's us get together everything we can for her."

And though hardly anybody in the village ever goes to anything two days in succession, they all said they'd come.

By the time they got there next day we had carpet to sew out of some of our attics, and some new sheets to make, and some white muslin curtains out of Mis' Puppy's back room. And I explained to them that we couldn't rightly put it to vote whether we should furnish up the Toll Gate House, because we didn't have any president to put the motion, so the only way was to go ahead anyhow and do it; which we done; and which, if not parlimental, was more than any mental, because it was out of our hearts.

Right while we was in the midst of things, in come my roomer, Mr. Dombledon. He'd come in the back door, as usual, and plumped into the sitting-room before he saw we were there. He'd had Donnie with him that day, because I had to be out most of the forenoon, and I called to them to stop, because I wanted the ladies should see the little fellow.

Donnie shook hands with us, all around, like a little general, and then: "What's these?" says he, with his hands on the curtains in my lap. "A nighty for me?"

"No, lambin'," says I. "It's curtains for a lady."

"Are you that lady?" he says.

"No, lambin'," says I. "A lady that ain't got any curtains."

But this he seemed to think was awful funny, and he laughed out—a little boy's laugh, and kep' it up.

"Ladies always has curtains," says he, superior.

"I donno," says I. "I saw one yesterday that didn't even have a carpet."

"Where?" asks Mr. Dombledon.

It kind of surprised me to hear him speak up—of course I'd introduced him all around, same as you do roomers and even agents in a little town, where you behave in general more as if folks were folks than you do in the City where they ain't so much folks as lawyers, ladies, milkmen, ministers, and so on. But yet I hadn't really expected Mr. Dombledon to volunteer.

"Down on the Tote road," I says, "the old Toll Gate House. You ain't familiar with it, I guess."

"Is this *hers* curtains?" asks Donnie. "And can I have some pink peaches sauce like in the kitchen?"

"They's *hers* curtains," says I, "and if you'd just as soon make it plums, you shall have all of them in the kitchen that's good for you." And off he went outdoors making up a song about pink plums.

All of a sudden his father spoke up again.

"Do—do you need any more help?" he says.

"Sure we do," says I.

"Well," he says, gentling with the words careful, "I'm kind of sure-moved with a needle."

"Then," says I, "mebbe you'll needle this carpet seam that's pulling my fingers off in pairs. We'd be grateful," says I, ready.

So down he sat and begun to sew, and I never see handier. He whipped up the seam as nice and flat as a roller machine. And things was going along as fine as salt and as smooth as soap when Mis' Puppy picked up from the pile of things a red cotton table-cover.

"Well," she says, "I donno where we solicited this from, but whoever give it shows their bringing up. Holes. And not only holes, but ink. And not only so, but look there where their lamp set. Would you think anybody of a donatin' mind would donate such a thing as this?"

And Mis' Pettibone spoke up sour and acid and bitter in one:

"I give that table-spread, Mis' Puppy," says she. "And it come off our dining-room table. We don't throw things away to our house before the new is wore off. Anything more to say?"

"A grea' deal," says Mis' Puppy, unflabbergasted, "but I'm too much of a lady to say it."

"A lady ..." says Mis' Pettibone, and done a little mock-at-her laugh.

Quick as a flash, and before anybody could say a word more, up hopped Mr. Dombledon and got out of the room. I followed him out on the side porch, thinking he was took sick; and there he stood, staring off acrost my wood lot.

"What is it, Mr. Dombledon?" I says.

"Don't you mind me," he says, "I got hit in a sore spot. I—guess I'll be stayin' out here a little while."

Pretty soon he went out and sat on the wood pile, and I took some supper out to him on a pie-tin, and I told him then that we wanted to have Donnie to the table with us.

He looked up at me kind of suffering.

"I wouldn't want to refuse you anything," he says, "but—will they say any more things like that?"

Right with the sweep of my wondering at him, that I'd never heard a man speak like him before, come a sweep of shame and of grieving and of being kind of mad, too.

"No, sir," says I. "We won't have any more of that. What's the good o' being hostess if you can't turn your guests out of the house?"

I went back into the house, and marched into the sitting-room. I donno what I was going to say, but I never had to say it. For there was Mis' Puppy, wiping her eyes on the red table-cover she'd scorned, and she was sitting on the arm of Mis' Pettibone's chair.

"Them things hadn't ought to be said, ladies," says she, as well as she could. "I can't take back what I said about the table-cover, being it's what I think. But I wish I'd kep' my mouth shut, and I don't care who knows it."

I thought then, and I still think, it was one of the honestest and sweepingest apologies I ever heard.

And all at once everybody kind of got up and folded their work, and patted somebody on the elbow; and I see we was feeling a good deal the way we had in the rig the night before; and it come to me, kind of big and dim, that with the job we was doing, we couldn't possibly nip out at one another, like we would in just regular society. And all I done was to sing out, "Your supper's ready and the toast's on the table." And we all went out, lion and lamb, and helped to set Donnie up on my ironing-stool for a high chair. And it made an awful pleasant few minutes.

We met three afternoons all together to sew for the Toll Gate House. And when we begun to plan to take the things to her, and get the roof mended, we realized we didn't know her name.

"Ain't that kind of nice?" says Mis' Pettibone, dreamy. "And here we're just as interested in her as if her father'd been our butcher, or something that'd make a real tie."

"How shall we give these things to her?" says Mis' Puppy. "Don't let's us let it be nasty, same as charity is."

And it was Mis' Lockmeyer, her of all the folks under the canopy, that set forward on the edge of her chair and thought of the thing to do. "Ladies," she says, "there's one more pair of curtains to hem. Why don't we get her to one of our houses to hem 'em, and make her spend the day? And get her roof fixed and her ceiling mended and this truck in, and let it all be there when she gets home?"

"That's what we *will* do," says we, with one set of common eyebrows expressing our intention.

We decided that I'd be the one to ask her down, being I was the one that first went in her house, and similar. She said she'd come ready enough, and bring the little girl; and it made it real convenient, because Mr. Dombledon had gone off on one of his two-days tramps and taken Donnie with him. And the living minute I'd started her in sewing on the things we'd saved for her to sew, and set the little girl to playing with some of the things I'd fixed up for Donnie, I was out of the house and making for the Toll Gate.

Land, land, the things we'd found we could spare and that we'd piled in that house—stuff that we hadn't known we had and that we couldn't miss if we'd tried, but had hung on to sole and only because we were deformed into economizing that way. Honestly, I believe more folks economizes by keeping old truck around than is extravagant by throwing new stuff away. I don't stand up for either, but I well know which has the most germs in. What we'd sent we'd cleaned thorough. And it was clean as wax there—but the roof was being mended and the ceiling was being fixed and carpets were going down. And when we got done with it, I tell you that little house looked as cozy as a Pullman car—and I don't know anything whatever that looks cozier after you've set up in the day coach all night. And lions and lambs laying down together on swords and plow-shares were nothing to the way we worked together all day long. We had to jump to keep out of the way of being "been-nice" to so's to get a chance to be nice ourselves. I liked to be there. I like to think about it since.

At five o'clock, old Mis' Lockmeyer, dead-tuckered, was standing in the door with a corner of her apron caught up in the band, when Jem drove me away.

"Leave her come out any time now," she says, "we're ready for her. Mebbe she'll be mad but, land—even if she is, I can't be sorry we done it. It's been as enjoyable," she says, "as anything I've ever done."

I looked back at her, and at all the other women back of her and in the windows, and at Mis' Pettibone and Mis' Puppy leaning on the same sill, and I nodded; and Mis' Puppy—well, it was faint and ladylike, but just the same the look that we give each other was far, far more than a squint, and it was bordering on, and right up to, a regular wink.

When I come in sight of my house I was so busy thinking how she'd like hers that I didn't see for a minute what my front yard had in it. And when I did see, my heart kind of went *plap!*—but a pleasant plap. My front yard looked so exactly the way I'd used to dream of it looking, and it never had. It was little and neat and green, with flowers and a white door-step as usual, but out in front was a little girl, with my clothes-rope doubled up for lines, and she was driving round and round the pansy bed a little boy. Just before I got to the gate, and before they saw me, they dropped the rope and went off around the house hand in hand, like they'd known each other all their days.

"I wish everybody was like that," thinks I, and went in my front door and through to the dining-room.

And there, sitting on my couch with their arms around each other, was the Toll Gate House lady and my roomer, Mr. Dombledon.

"Well," says I. "Sudden—but real friendly!"

I see I had to say something, for they didn't seem real capable of it. And besides, I'd begun to suspicion, deep in the part of the heart that ain't never surprised at love anywheres.

Mr. Dombledon come over to me—and now his eyes were like the sitting-room with all the curtains up.

"Oh, ma'am!" he says, "how did you know? How did you find out?"

"Know?" I says. "I know less all the time. And I ain't found out yet. I'm a-waiting for you to tell me."

"We're each other's wife and husband," says he, neat but shy.

They told me as well as they could, now together, now separate, now both keeping still. I made it out more by means of the air than by means of words, anyhow. But this thing that he said came home to me then, and it's never left me since:

"Nothin' come between us," he says. "No great trouble or sorrow or like that, same as some. It was just every day that wore us out. We got to snappin' and snarlin'—like you do. We done it at everything—whenever either of us opened our heads, the other one took 'em up on it. We done it because we was tired. And we done it because we didn't have much to do with—nor no real home. And we done it for no reason too, I guess ... an' that come to be the oftenest of all. It got hold of us. That was what ailed me that day at your meeting—I'd always run from it now same as I would from the pest. It *is* the pest.... Well, finally I went off with Donnie and left Pearl with her. Then when I found out she'd come here, I come here too, a-purpose. But I couldn't go and face her, even then. And it's been six months. And now we both know."

I stood there looking at those two little people, shabby and or'nary-seeming; and I could have said something right past the lump in my throat if only I could of thought how to put it. But I couldn't—like you can't. Only—I knew.

"Where is he?" I heard her saying. "Where is he?"

I knew who she meant, and I went and got him. He come running in with his swing-board on him for a breast-plate. And his mother never said a word—she just gathered him up, swing-board and all, and kissed him at the back of his neck, there in the hollow that had been a-waiting for her.

"She made me cookies wiv buttins on!" he give out, for my biography. And it was enough for me.

Mr. Dombledon had his little girl's hands in his, swinging her arms back and forth, and never saying a word.

Pretty soon I sent 'em off down the road, Donnie and Pearl ahead, they two behind, carrying my ex-roomer's things. And I knew how, at the Toll Gate House, everything was warm and bright and furnished and *suppered*, waiting for them. And life was nice.

I went and stood out on my porch, looking off acrost my wood lot, thinking. I was thinking about the two of them, and about us women. And I knew I'd been showed the little bit of an edge to something that's so small it don't seem like anything, and so sordid we won't any of us let on it comes near us, and so big it reaches all over the world.

HUMAN

PRETTY soon the new-old Christmas will be here. I donno but it's here now. Here in the village we've give out time and again that our Christmas isn't going to be just trading (not many of us can call it "shopping" yet without stopping to think, any more than we can say "maid" for hired girl, real easy) and just an exchange of useless gifts. So in the "new" way, little by little the old Christmas is being uncovered from under the store-keepers' Christmas. Till at last we shall have the Christmas of the child in the manger and not of the three kings.

And then we're going to look back on the romance that Christmas had through the long time when meanings have measured themselves commercial. Just as we look back now on the romance of chivalry. And we'll remember all the kindness and the humor of the time that'll be outgrown—even though we wouldn't have the time come back when we looked for Christmas in things—things—things ... and sometimes found it there.

The week before Christmas, the Friendship Village post-office, near closing, is regular Bedlam. We all stand in line, with our presents done up, while the man at the window weighs everybody else's, and we almost drop in our tracks. And our manners, times like this, is that we never get out of our place for no one. Not for no one! Only—once we did.

Two nights before Christmas that year I got my next-to-the-last three packages ready and stepped into the post-office with 'em about half-past seven. And at the post-office door I met Mis' Holcomb-that-was-Mame Bliss. She had a work-bag and a shopping-bag and a suit-case, all of 'em bulging full.

"My land!" I says, "you ain't going to mail all them?"

"I am, too," she says, "and I'm that thankful I'm through, and my back aches that hard, I could cry. Twenty-one," she says, grim, "twenty-one presents I've got made out of thought and elbow work, and mighty little money, all ready to mail on time. Now," says she, "I can breathe."

"Kin I carry your satchel, Mis' Holcomb?" says somebody.

We looked down, and there's little Stubby Mosher, that's seven, and not much else to say about him. He ain't no father, nor not much of any brother, except a no-account one in the city; and his mother has just been sent to the Wooster Hospital by the Cemetery Improvement Sodality that is extending our work to include the sick. We'd persuaded her to go there by

Stubby's brother promising to send him to spend Christmas with her. And we were all feeling real tender toward Stubby, because we'd just heard that week that she wasn't going to get well.

"Well, Stubby," says Mis' Holcomb, kind, "yes, I'll be obliged for a lift, if not a lug. You well?" she asks.

"Yes'm," says Stubby, acting green, like a boy will when you ask after his health.

He picked up her suit-case and moved over toward the line. It was an awful long line that night, that reached 'way around past the public desk. In ahead of us was 'most everybody we knew—Abigail Arnold and Mis' Merriman and Libby Liberty and old rich Mis' Wiswell with a bag of packages looking like they might be jewelry, every one. And every one of them was talking as hard as they could about the Christmas things they couldn't get done.

"Might as well settle down for a good visit while we're waiting," I says to Mis' Holcomb, and she made her eyebrows sympathize.

No sooner was we stood up, neat and in line, than in come three folks that was total strangers to me and to the village as well. One was a young girl around twenty, with eyes kind of laughing *at* everything, dressed in blue, with ermine on her hat and an ermine muff as big as one of my spare-room pillows, and three big fresh pink roses on her coat. And one was a youngish fellow, some older than her, in a gray cap, and having no use of his eyes—being they were kept right close on the lady in blue. And the other, I judged, was her father—a nice, jolly, private Santa Claus, in a fur-lined coat. They were in a tearing hurry to get to the general-delivery window, but when they saw the line, and how there was only one window for mail and stamps and all, they fell in behind us, as nice as we was ourselves.

"Let me take you out and you wait in the car, Alison," says the youngish man, anxious.

"Hadn't you better, dear?" says her father, careful.

"Why, but I love this!" she says. "Isn't it *quaint?*" And she laughed again.

Now, I hate that word *quaint*. So does Mis' Holcomb. It always sounds to us like last year's styles. So though her and I had been looking at the three strangers—that we saw were merely passing through in an automobile, like the whole country seems to—with some interest, we both turned our backs and went on visiting and listening to the rest.

"I've got three more to get presents for," says Mis' Merriman in that before-Christmas conversation that everybody takes a hand at, "and what to get them I do *not* know. Don't you ever get up a stump about presents?"

"Stump!" says Libby Liberty, "I live on a stump from the time I start till I stick on the last stamp."

"I've got two more on my list," Mis' Wiswell says, worried, "and it don't seem as if I could take another stitch nor buy another spoon, hat-pin *or* paper-knife. But I know they'll send me something, both of them."

I stood looking at us, tired to death with what we'd been a-making, but sending 'em off with a real lot of love and satisfaction wrapped up in 'em, too. And I thought how we covered up Christmas so deep with work that we hardly ever had time to get at the real Christmas down underneath all the stitches. And yet, there we were, having dropped everything else that we were doing, just because it was Christmas week, and coming from all over town with little things we had made, and standing there in line to send 'em off to folks. And I thought of all the other folks in all the other post-offices in the world, doing the self-same thing that night. And I felt all kind of nice and glowing to think I was one of 'em. Only I did begin to wish we were enough civilized to get the glow some other way.

"I guess it's going to take a long time," says Mis' Holcomb, patient. "Stubby, you needn't wait if you've anything else to do."

"Oh," says Stubby, important, "I've got a present to mail."

A present to mail! When Sodality had been feeding him for five weeks among us!

Mis' Holcomb and I exchanged our next two glances.

"What is it, Stubby?" asks Mis' Holcomb, that is some direct by nature and never denies herself at it.

He looked up kind of shy—he's a nice little boy, when anybody has any time to pay any attention to him.

"It's just this," he said, and took it out from under his coat. It was about as big as a candy box, and he'd wrapped it up himself, and the string was so loose and the paper was so tore that they weren't going to stay by each other past two stations.

"Mercy!" says Mis' Holcomb, "leave me tie it up for you."

She took it. And in order to tie it she had to untie it. And when she done that, what was in it come all untied. And she see, and we both of us see, what was in it. It was a great big pink rose, fresh and real, with a lot of soaking wet paper wrapped round the stem.

"Stubby Mosher!" says Mis' Holcomb straight out, "where'd *you* get this?"

He colored up. "I bought it to the greenhouse," he says. "I'm a-goin' to shovel paths till the first of March to pay for it. And they gimme one path ahead for postage."

"Who you sending it to?" says Mis' Holcomb, blunt—and I kind of wished she wouldn't, because the folks right round us was beginning to listen.

"To mother," says Stubby.

Mis' Holcomb near dropped the box. "My land!" she said, "why didn't you *take* it to her? You're goin' to-morrow to spend Christmas with her, ain't you?"

Stubby shook his head and swallowed some.

"I ain't going," he told her.

"Ain't going!" Mis' Holcomb says. "*Why* ain't you goin', I'd like to know, when you was promised?"

"My brother wrote he can't," said Stubby. "He's had some money to pay. He can't send me. I——"

He stopped, and looked down on the floor as hard as ever he could, and swallowed like lightning.

"Well, but that's how we got her to go there," Mis' Holcomb says. "We promised her you'd come."

"My brother wrote he can't." Stubby said it over.

Mis' Holcomb looked at me for just one minute. Then her thoughts took shape in her head, and out.

"How much money has Sodality got in the treasury?" she says to me.

"Forty-six cents," says I, that's treasurer and drove to death for a fund for us.

"How much is the fare to Wooster?"

"Three fifty-five each way," says Stubby, ready, but hopeless.

"My land!" says Mis' Holcomb, "they ain't a woman in Sodality that can afford the seven dollars—nor a man in the town'll see it like we do. And no time to raise nothing. And that poor woman off there...."

She stared out over the crowd, kind of wild.

The line was edging along up to the window, and still talking about it.

"...Elsie and Mame that I haven't sent a thing to," Mis' Merriman was saying. "I just must get out and find something to-morrow, if it does get there late. But I'm sure I donno what...."

"...disappointed me last minute on two Irish crochet collars," Mis' Wiswell was holding forth, in her voice that talks like her vocal cords had gone flat, same as car-wheels.

"I've got company coming to-morrow, and I just simply will *have* to let both presents go, if I stay awake all night about it, as stay awake I s'pose I shall."

Mis' Holcomb looked over at me steady for a minute, like she'd see a thing she couldn't name. Then she kind of give it up, and went on tying Stubby's package. And just then she see what he'd wrote for a Christmas card. It was on a piece of wrapping-paper, and it said:

TO MY MOTHER
I CANT COM
MERY CRISMAS
STUB

"*Merry Christmas!*" Mis' Holcomb says over like she hadn't any strength. Then all of a sudden she stood up.

"Stubby," she says, "you run out a minute, will you? You run over to the grocery and wait for me there a minute—quick. I'll see to your package."

He went when she said that.

And swift as a flash, before I could think at all what she meant, Mis' Holcomb laid Stubby's present down by her suit-case, and wheeled around and whipped two packages out of her shopping-bag, and faced the line of Friendship Village folks drawn up there to the window, taking their turns.

"Everybody!" she says, loud enough so's they all heard her, "I've got more Christmas presents than I need. I'll auction off some of 'em—all hand-made—to anybody that's short of presents. I'll show 'em to you. Come here and look at 'em, and make a bid."

They looked at her for a minute, perfectly blank; and she was beginning to undo one of 'em.... And then all of a sudden I see her plan, what it was; and I walked right over beside of her.

"Don't you leave her undo 'em!" I calls out. "It's for Stubby Mosher," I says, "that can't go, after all, to his mother in the Wooster Hospital, that's going to die—count of his brother not sending him the money. She can't get well—we know that since last week. They's only forty-six cents in Sodality treasury. Let's us buy Mis' Holcomb's presents that she's made and is willing to auction off! Unsight-unseen let us buy 'em! I bid fifty cents."

The line had kind of wavered and broke, and was looking away from itself towards us. The man at the window had stopped weighing and had his head close up, looking out.

Everybody was hushed dumb for a minute. Then it kind of got to Mis' Wiswell—that's had so much trouble that things 'most always get to her easy—and she says out:

"Oh, land! *Is it?* Why, I bid seventy-five then."

"Eighty!" says I, reckless, to egg her on.

Then Libby Liberty kind of come to, and bid ninety, though everybody knew the most she has is egg-money—and finally it, whatever it was, went to Mis' Wiswell for a dollar.

"Is it a present would do for ladies?" she says, when she made her final bid. "I donno, though, as that matters. One dollar!"

Well, then Mis' Holcomb up with another present, and Mis' Merriman started that one, and though dazed a little yet—some folks daze so terrible easy if you go off an inch from their stamping-ground!—the rest of us, including Abigail Arnold that hadn't ought to have bid at all, got that one up to another dollar, and it went to Mis' Merriman for that. But the next package stuck at fifty cents—not from lack of willingness, I know, but from sheer lack of ways—and it was just going at that when I whispered to Mis' Holcomb:

"What's in this one?"

"Towel with crochet work set in each end and no initial," she says.

"Really?" says a voice behind me.

And there was the young lady in blue, with the ermine and the roses. And I see all of a sudden that she didn't look to be laughing at us at all, but her eyes were bright, and she was kind of flushed up, and it come to me that she would have bidded before, only she was sort of watching us—

mebbe because she thought we were *quaint*. But I didn't have time to bother with that thought much, not then.

"I'll give two dollars for that," she says.

"Done!" says Mis' Holcomb, real auctioneer-like, and with her cheeks red, and her hat on one ear, and her hand going up and down. "Now this one—who'll bid on this one?" says she, putting up another. "How much for this? How much——"

"How much is the fare to where he's going?" says somebody else strange, and there was the youngish fellow speaking, that was with her with the roses.

"Seven-ten round trip to Wooster," says Mis' Holcomb, instant.

"Why, then, I bid three-ten for whatever you have there," he says laughing.

But Mis' Holcomb, instead of flaming up because now the whole money for Stubby's fare was raised, just stood there looking at that youngish man, mournful all over her face.

"It's a hand-embroidered dressing-sack," she says melancholy. "You don't never want that!"

"Yes—yes, I do," he says, still laughing, "yes, I do. It's a straight bid."

"Oh, my land!" says Mis' Holcomb, her voice slipping, "then we've got it. We've got it all right here!"

But while she was a-saying it, a big, deep voice boomed out all over her and the rest that was exclaiming.

"Ticket to where?" says the private-Santa-Claus-looking man in the fur coat.

"Wooster, this state," says I, being Mis' Holcomb was almost speechless.

"Well, now," says the private Santa Claus, "don't we go pretty close to Wooster? Where's that map we wore out? Well, I know we go pretty close to Wooster. Why can't we take your Master Stubby to Wooster in the car? We're going on to-night—if we ever get to that general-delivery window," he ends in a growl.

And *that* was the time the line made way—the line that never moves for no one. And the Santa Claus man went up and got his mail.

And while he was a-doing it, I run out after Stubby, setting on a barrel in the grocery, happy with three cranberries they'd give him. And as I come back in the door with him, I see Mis' Holcomb just showing his rose to the young lady with the ermine and the roses. And then I see for sure by the young lady's eyes that she wasn't the way I'd thought she was—laughing *at* us. Why, her eyes were as soft and understanding as if she didn't have a cent to her name. And I donno but more so.

"Oh, father," I heard her say, "I'm glad we came in for the mail ourselves! *What* if we hadn't?"

And I concluded I didn't mind that word *quaint* half as much as I thought I did.

Every last one of the line went out of the post-office to see Stubby off, and the man at the window, he came too. They had a big warm coat they put the little boy into, and we wrapped up his rose and put that in the car, so's it would get there sooner and save the postage, same time, and they tucked him away as snug as a bug in a rug, his little face just shining out for joy.

"Oh, and you can buy your presents back now," says Libby Liberty to Mis' Holcomb right in the middle of it.

"No, sir," says Mis' Holcomb, proud. "A bargain is a bargain, and I made mine." And then she thought of something. "Oh," she says, leaning forward to the window of the car, "don't you want to sell your presents back again?"

"No!" they all told her together. "We made a straight bid, you know."

"*Then*," says Mis' Holcomb, "let's us give Stubby the money to put in his pocket and take the one-way fare to his mother!"

And that was what they done. And the big car rolled off down Daphne Street, with Stubby in it going like a king.

And when we all got back in the post-office, what do you s'pose? There was the crocheted towel and the hand-embroidered dressing-sack slipped back all safe into Mis' Holcomb's shopping-bag!

But she wouldn't take the other things back—she would not, no matter what Mis' Wiswell and Mis' Merriman said.

"I can crochet a couple of things to-morrow like lightning," says Mis' Holcomb. "You don't want me to be done out of my share in Stubby's Christmas, do you?" she asks 'em.

And we all stood there, talking and laughing and going over it and clean forgetting all about the United States mails, till the man at the window called out:

" 'Leven minutes and a quarter before the mail closes!"

We all started back to the window, but nobody could remember just exactly where anybody was standing before, and they all wanted everybody to go up first and step in ahead of them. And the line, instead of being a line with some of 'em ahead of others and all trying to hurry, was just a little group, with each giving everybody their turn, peaceful and good-willing. And all of a sudden it was like Christmas had come, up through all the work and the stitches, and was right there in the Friendship Village post-office with us.

"Goodness!" says Mis' Holcomb in my ear, "I was wore to the bone getting ready my Christmas things. But now I'm real rested."

"So am I," I says.

And so was every one of us, I know, falling back into line there by the window. All rested, and not feeling hurried nor nothing: only human.

THE HOME-COMING

"Eighteen booths," says Mis' Timothy Toplady, sighing satisfied. "That's enough to go round the whole Market Square, leaving breathin' space between."

We sat looking at the diagram Mis' Fire-Chief Merriman had made on the dining-room table, with bees-wax and stuff out of her work-basket, and we all sighed satisfied—but tired too. Because, though it looked like the Friendship Village Home-coming was going to be a success—and a peaceful success—yet we see in the same flash that it was going to be an awful back-aching, feet-burning business for us ladies. We were having our fourth committee meeting to Mis' Sykes's, and we weren't more than begun on the thing; and the Home-coming was only six weeks away.

"Just thinking about all the tracking round it means," says Mis' Sykes, "I can feel that sick feeling in the back of my throat *now*, that I feel when I'm over-tired, or got delegates, or have company pounce down on me."

Mis' Hubbelthwait looked at her sympathetic. "I know," she says. "So tired you can taste it. I donno," she says, "whether home-comings are worth it or not."

Mis' Sykes didn't answer. She was up on her feet, peering out behind the Nottinghams.

"My land o' life," she says, "that's the stalkin' image of 'Lisbeth Note."

"Lisbeth *Note*!" we all said. "Oh, it can't be!"

It struck me, even then, how united folks are on a piece of gossip. For the Home-coming some had thought have printed invitations and some had thought send out newspapers, some had wanted free supper and some had wanted pay, and so on, item by item of the afternoon. But the minute Lisbeth Note was mentioned, we all burst into one common, spontaneous fraternal horror: "*Oh, no.* It couldn't be her."

"It is!" cries Mis' Sykes. "It is. She's turning in there. I thought I heard 'bus wheels in the night. It serves me right. I'd ought to got out and looked."

We were all crowded to the window by then, looking over toward old Mis' Note's, that lived opposite to Mis' Sykes's. So we all saw what we saw. And it was that Mis' Note's front door opened and a little boy, 'bout four years old, come shouting down the walk toward Lisbeth. And she stooped over and kissed him. And they went in the house together and shut the door.

Then us ladies turned and stared at each other. And Mis' Sykes says, swallowing unbeknownst in the middle of what she says: "The brazen hussy. She's brought it back here."

I donno whether you've ever heard a group of immortal beings, women or men, pounce on and mull over *that* particular bone? If you live somewheres in this world, I guess mebbe you hev—I guess mebbe you hev. I'm never where it happens, that I don't turn sick and faint all through me. I don't know how men handles the subject—here in Friendship Village we don't mention things that has a tang to 'em, in mixed company. Mebbe men is delicate and gentle and chivalrous when they speak of such things. Mebbe that's one of the places they use the chivalry some feels so afraid is going to die out. But I might as well own up to you that in Friendship Village us women don't act neither delicate nor decent in such a case.

There was fourteen women in the room that day, every one of 'em except Abigail Arnold and me living what you might call "protected" lives. I mean by that that men had provided them their homes and was earning them their livings, and clothing their children; and they were caring for the man's house and, in between, training up the children. Then we were all of us further protected by the church, that we all belonged to and helped earn money for. And also we were protected by the town, that we were all respectable, bill-paying, property-owning, pew-renting citizens of. That was us.

And over against us fourteen was Lisbeth—that her father had died when she was a baby, and her mother had worked since she was born, with no place to leave Lisbeth meantime. And Lisbeth herself had been a nice, sweet-dispositioned, confiding little girl, doing odd jobs to our houses and clerking in our stores in the Christmas rush. Till five years ago—she'd gone away. And we all knew why. Her mother had cried her eyes out in most every one of our kitchens, and we were all in full possession of the facts—unless you count in the name of the little child's father. We didn't know that. But then, we had so much to do tearing Lisbeth to pieces we didn't bother a great deal with that. And there that day was the whole fourteen of us, pitching into Lisbeth Note for what she'd done—just like she was fourteen of herself, our own sizes and our own "protectedness," and meeting us face to face.

"The *idea!*" says Mis' Sykes, shaking her head, with her lips disappearing within her face. "Why, she might have been clerking in the post-office store now, a nice, steady, six-dollar-a-week position just exactly like she was when it happened."

"Would you think," says Mis' Fire-Chief Merriman, "that living here in Friendship Village with us, anybody *could* go wrong?"

"Sepulchers in sheep's clothing—that's what some folks are," says little new Mis' Graves, righteous.

And so on. And on. Hashing it all over again and eating it for cake. And me, I wasn't silent either. I joined in here and there with a little something I'd heard. Till by the time the meeting adjourned, and we'd all agreed to meet two days later and sew on the bunting for the booths, I went home feeling so sick and hurt and sore and skinned that after dark I up and walked straight down to Lisbeth's house. Yes. After dark. I was a poor, weak, wavering stick, and I knew it.

Lisbeth came to the door. "Hello, Lisbeth," I says. "It's Calliope Marsh. Can I come in?"

"Mother ain't here, Mis' Marsh," she says faint.

"Ain't she, now?" I says. "I bet she is. I'm going inside to hunt for her."

And I walked right into the sitting-room and turned and looked at Lisbeth. If she'd been defiant, or acted don't-care, or tossed her head, or stared at me—I donno's I'd of had the strength to understand that these might be her poor, pitiful weapons. But as it was, her eyes looked straight into mine for a minute, and then brimmed up full of tears. So I kissed her.

We sat there for an hour in the twilight—an hour I'll never forget. And then she took me up-stairs to show me the boy.

Think of the prettiest child you know. Think of the prettiest child you ever did know. Now think of him laying asleep, all curls and his cheeks flushed and his lips budded open a little bit. That was Chris. That was Little Christopher—Lisbeth's little boy.

"Miss Marsh," Lisbeth says, "I'd rather die than not have him with me. And mother ain't strong, and she needs me. Do you think I done wrong to come home?"

"Done wrong?" I says. "Done wrong to come home? Don't them words kind of fight each other in the sentence? Of course you didn't do wrong. Why," says I, "Lisbeth, this is Friendship Village's Home-coming year. It's Home-coming week next month, you know."

She looked at me wistful there in the dark beside the child's bed. "Oh, not for me," she says. "This house is my home—but this town ain't any more. It don't want me."

"It don't want me," I says over to myself, going home. And I looked along at the nice, neat little houses, with the front doors standing open to the spring night, and dishes clattering musical here and there in kitchens, getting washed up, and lights up-stairs where children were being put to bed. And I thought, "Never tell me that this little town don't want everybody that belongs to it to live in it. The town is true. It's folks that's false." I says that over: "The town is true. It's folks that's false. How you going to make them know it?"

When it come my turn to have the Homecoming committee meet to my house, things had begun to get exciting. Acceptances had commenced coming in. I'd emptied out my photograph basket, and we had 'em all in it. It was real fun and heart-warming to read 'em. Miss Sykes was presiding—that woman'll be one of them that comes back from the grave to do table-rapping. She does so love to call anything to order.

"Judge Eustis Bangs is coming," says Mis' Sykes, impressive, looking over the envelopes. "They say his wife don't think anything in the world of having company in to a meal every week or so."

" 'Used-to' Bangs coming!" cries Mis' Holcomb-that-was-Mame Bliss. "He set behind me in school. Land, I ain't seen him since graduating exercises when he dipped my braid in the inkwell."

"And Sarah Arthur," Mis' Sykes went on. "She's lady bookkeeper in a big department store in the city, and in with all them four hundred."

"I always wonder," says Mis' Holcomb, looking up and frowning meditative, "four hundred *what*? Do they mean folks, or millionaires, or what do they mean by that?"

"Oh, why millionaires, of course," says Mis' Sykes. "It don't refer to *folks*. Look-a-here," she says next. "Admiral and Mrs. Homer is coming. Why, you know he was only bare born here—he went away before he was three months old. And she's never been here. But they're coming now. Ladies! A admiral!"

Mis' Toplady had been sitting still over in one corner, darning, with her mind on it. But now she dropped her husband's sock, and looked up. "Admiral," she says over. "That's something to do with water fighting, ain't it? Well, I want to know what they call it that for? I thought we didn't consider it admiral any more to kill folks, by land or by sea?"

"Oh, but he's an officer," Mis' Sykes says worshipful. "He'll have badges, and like enough pantalettes on his shoulders; and think how nice he'll look heading the parade!"

Mis' Toplady kind of bit at her darning-needle, dreamy. "To my mind," she says, "the only human being that's fit to head a parade is one that's just old enough to walk."

Just then Mis' Sykes done her most emphatic squeal and pucker, such as, if she was foreign, she would reserve for royalty alone.

"My land," she says, "Abner Dawes! He's a-coming. He's a-*coming*!"

There couldn't have been a nicer compliment to any one, my way of thinking, than the little round of smiles and murmurs that run about among us when we heard this.

Abner Dawes had been, thirty years before, a nice, shy man round the village, and we all liked him, because he had such a nice, kind way with him and particularly because he had such a way with children. He used to sing 'em little songs he made up. And some of the little songs got in the paper and got copied in the city paper; and first thing we knew, a big firm sent for Abner, and he'd been gone ever since. We heard of him, now doing his children-songs on the stage, now in a big, beautiful book of children's songs, with pictures, that had been sent back to the village. And we were prouder of him than 'most anybody we'd got. And here he was coming to the Home-coming.

"We must give him the Principal Place, whatever that is," says Mis' Sykes, immediate. And we all agreed. Yes, Abner must have the Principal Place.

We were sewing, that afternoon, on the bunting for Eppleby Holcomb's store's booth. Blazing red, it was—ain't it queer how men loves red? Color of blood and color of fire; but I always think it means they'll be ready to love not blood of war but blood-brotherhood, and not the torch to burn with, but the torch to light with—when the time comes. Yes, I bet men's liking red means something, and I like to think it means that. And if it does, Eppleby'll be first among men, for he didn't want a stitch of his booth that wasn't flaming scarlet.

We had the diagram all made out on the table again, so's to tell what colors would come next to which. And all of a sudden Mis' Sykes put her finger in the middle of it.

"Do you know what?" she says. "If that tree wasn't in the middle there, we could have a great big evening bon-fire, with everybody around it."

"So we could. Wouldn't that be nice?" says everybody—only me. Because the tree they meant was the Christmas tree, the big evergreen, the living Christmas tree that had stood there in the square, all lit, that last Christmas Eve, with all of us singing round it.

"I can't ever think of that being in anybody's way," I says, and everybody says, "Perhaps not," and we went on tearing off the lengths of blazing red calico. And me, I set there thinking about what they'd said.

I remember I was still thinking about it, and Mis' Sykes and I were standing up together measuring off the breadths, when the front door opened. And there was standing Chris, Lisbeth's little boy. Him and I'd got to be awful good friends almost from the first. He come over to my house quite a lot, and kneeled on a chair side of the table when I was doing my baking, and he brought me in pans of chips. And no little fellow whatever was ever sweeter.

"Hello, dear," I says now. "Come in, won't you?"

He stood quiet, eying us. And Mis' Sykes down she drops the cloth and made a dive for him.

"You darling!" says she—her emphasis coming out in bunches, the way some women's does when they talk to children. "You darling! *Whose* little boy are you?"

He looked at her, shy and sweet. "I'm my mamma's little boy," he says, ready. "But my papa, he didn't come—not yet."

I looked over to Mis' Sykes, squatting with both arms around the baby. "He's Lisbeth's little boy," I says. "Ain't he d-e-a-r?"—I spells it.

Mis' Sykes drew back, like the little fellow had hit at her. "Mercy!" she says, only—and got up, and went on tearing cloth.

He felt it, like little children do feel ever so much more than we know they feel. I see his little lip begin to curl. I went and whispered that we'd go find an orange in the pantry, and I took him to get it; and then he went off.

When I went back in the sitting-room they all kind of kept still, like they'd been saying things they didn't mean I should hear. Only that little new Mis' Morgan Graves, she sat with her back to the door and she was speaking.

"...for one Sunday. But when I found it out, I took Bernie right out of the class. Of course it don't matter so much now, but when they get older, you can't be too careful."

I went and stood back of her chair.

"Oh, yes, you can," says I. (We try here in Friendship Village not to contradict our guests too flat; but when it's a committee meeting, of course a hostess feels more free.) "You can be a whole lot too careful," I went on. "You can be so careful that you act like we wasn't all seeds in one great big patch of earth, same as we are."

"Well, but, Calliope," says Mis' Sykes, "you can't take that child in. You ain't any children, or you'd know how a mother feels. An illegitimate child——"

Then I boiled over and sissed on the tip of the stove. "Stop that!" I says. "Chris ain't any more illegitimate than I am. True, he's got a illegitimate father bowing around somewheres in polite society. And Lisbeth—well, she's bore him and she's raised him and she's paid his keep for four years, and I ain't prepared to describe what kind of mother she is by any one word in the dictionary. But the minute you tack that one word on to Chris, well," says I, "you got me to answer to."

"But, Calliope!" cries Mis' Sykes. "You can't take *him* in without taking in the mother!"

"No," says I, "and I've took her in already. Is my morals nicked any to speak of? Mind you," I says, "I ain't arguin' with you to take in anybody up till they want to be took in and do right. I've got my own ideas on that too, but I ain't arguing it with you here. All I say now is, Why *not* take in Lisbeth?"

"Why not put a premium on evil-doing and have done with it?" says Mis' Fire-Chief Merriman, majestic and deep-toned.

"Well," I says, "we've done that to the father's evil. Maybe you can tell me why we fixed up his premium so neat?"

"Oh, well," says Mis' Sykes, "surely we needn't argue it. Why, the whole of civilization is on our side and responsible for our way of thinking. You ain't got no argument, Calliope," she says. "Besides, it ain't what any of us thinks that proves it. It's what's what that counts."

"Civilization," says I. "And time. They're responsible for a good deal, ain't they? Wars and martyrdom and burnings and—crucifixion. All done in the immortal name of what's what. Well, me, I don't care a cake o' washing soap what's what. What's what ain't nothing but a foot-bridge anyhow, on over to what's-going-to-be. And if you tell me that civilization and time can keep going much longer putting a premium on a man's wrong and putting a penalty on the woman—then I tell you to your face that I've got inside information that you ain't got. Because in the end—in the end, *life ain't that sort.*"

"Good for you, Calliope!" says a voice in the door. And when I'd wheeled round, there stood Eppleby Holcomb, come in to see how we were getting along with the cloth for his booth. "Good for you," he says, grave.

We all felt stark dumb with embarrassment—I guess they hadn't one of us ever said that much in company with a man present in our lives. In company, with man or men present, we'd talked like life was made up of the pattern of things, and like speaking of warp and woof wasn't delicate. And we never so much as let on they *was* any knots—unless it was property knots or like that. But now I had to say something, being I had said something. And besides, I wanted to.

"Do you believe that too, Eppleby?" I ask' him breathless. "Do any men believe that?"

"Some men do, thank God," Eppleby says. And his wife, Mame, smiled over to him; and Mis' Timothy Toplady, she booms out: "Yes, *let's* thank God!" And I see that anyhow we four felt one. And "Is this stuff for my blazing booth here?" Eppleby sings out, to relieve the strain. And we all talked at once.

From that day on it seemed as if the whole town took sides about Lisbeth.

Half of 'em talked like Mis' Sykes, often and abundant. And one-quarter didn't say much of anything till they were pressed to. And the remaining one-quarter didn't say anything for fear of offending the other three-fourths, here and there. But some went to see Lisbeth, and sent her in a little something. She didn't go much of anywheres—she was shy of accepting pity where it would embarrass the givers. But oh my, how she did need friends!

Mame Holcomb was the only one that Lisbeth went to her house by invite. Mame let it be known that she had invited her, and full half of them she'd asked sent in their regrets in consequence. And of them that did go—well, honest, of all the delicate tasks the Lord has intrusted to His blundering children, I think the delicatest is talking to one of us that's somehow stepped off the track in public.

I heard Mis' Morgan Graves trying to talk to Lisbeth about like this: "My *dear* child. *How* do you get on?"

"Very nice, thank you, Mis' Graves," says Lisbeth.

"Is there *any*thing I can do to help you?" the lady pursues, earnest.

"No, Mis' Graves, nothing—thank you," says Lisbeth, looking down.

"You know I'd be so willing, so *very* willing, to do all I could at any time. You feel that about me, don't you?"

"Yes, ma'am," says Lisbeth, beginning to turn fire red.

"Promise," says Mis' Graves, "to let me know if you ever need a friend——"

And I couldn't stand it a minute longer. "That's you, Mis' Graves," I broke in hearty. "And it's what I've been wanting to say to you for ever so long. You're a good soul. Whenever you need a friend, just come to me. Will you?"

She looked kind of dazed, and three-fourths indignant. "Why ..." she begun.

And I says: "And you'd let me come to you if I need a friend, wouldn't you? I thought so. Well, now, here's three of us good friends, and showing it only when it's needed. Let's us three go and set down together for refreshments, sha'n't we?"

Lisbeth looked up at me like a dog that I'd patted. I donno but Mis' Graves thought I was impertinent. I donno but I was. But I like to be—like that. Oh, anything but the "protected" women that go cooing and humming and pooring around a girl like Lisbeth, and doing it in the name of friendliness. Friendliness isn't that. And if you don't know what it is different from that, then go out into the crowd of the world, stripped and hungry and dumb and by yourself, and wait till it comes to you. It'll come! God sees to that. And it's worth everything. For if you die without finding it out, you die without knowing life.

After that day, none of us invited Lisbeth in company. We see it was kinder not to.

But the little boy—the little boy. There wasn't any way of protecting him. And it never entered Lisbeth's head at first that she was going to be struck at through him. She sent him to Sunday-school, and everything was all right there, except Mis' Graves taking her little boy out of the class he was in, and Lisbeth didn't know that. Then she sent him to day school, in the baby room. And Mis' Sykes's little grandchild went there—Artie Barling; and I guess he must have heard his mother and Mis' Sykes talking—anyway at recess he shouts out when they was playing:

"Everybody that was born in the house be on my side!"

They all went rushing over to his side, Christopher too.

"Naw!" Artie says to him. "*Not* youse. Youse was borned *outside*. My gramma says so."

So Chris went home, crying, with that. And then Lisbeth begun to understand. I went in to see her one afternoon, and found her working out in the little patch of her mother's garden. When she see me she set down by the hollyhocks she was transplanting and looked up at me, just numb.

"Miss Marsh," she says, "it's God punishing me, I s'pose, but———"

"No, Lisbeth," I says. "No. The real punishment ain't this. This is just folks punishing you. Don't never mistake the one for the other, will you?"

Acceptances to the Home-coming kept flowing in like mad—all the folks we'd most wanted to come was a-coming, them and their families. I begun to get warm all through me, and to go round singing, and to wake up feeling something grand was going to happen and, when I was busy, to know there was something nice, just over the edge of my job, sitting there rosy, waiting to be thought about. It worked on us all that way. It was a good deal like being in love. I donno but it was being in love. In love with folks.

The afternoon before the Home-coming was to begin, there was to be a rehearsal of the Children's Drill, that Mis' Sykes had charge of for the opening night. We were all on the Market Square, working like beavers and like trojums, or whatever them other busy animals are, getting the booths set up. All the new things that the town had got and done in the last fifty years was represented, each in a booth, all round the Square.... And in the middle of the Square stood the great big Cedar-of-Lebanon tree that we'd used last Christmas for the first annual Friendship Village outdoors Christmas tree. I wondered how anybody could ever have said that it was in the way! It stood there, all still, and looking like it knew us far, far better than we knew it—the way a tree does. With the wind blowing through it gentle, it made a wonderful nice center-piece, I thought.

We'd just got to tacking on to Eppleby Holcomb's red Department Emporium booth when we heard a shout, and there, racing along the street, come the forty-fifty children that was going to be in the Children's Drill. They all come pounding and scampering over to where we were, each with a little paper stick in their hand for the wand part, and they swarmed up to Mis' Sykes that was showing 'em how, and they shouted:

"Mis' Sykes! Mis' Sykes! Can't we rehearse now?"—for "rehearse" seems to be a word that children just loves by natural instinct same as "cave" and "den" and "secret stairway."

I looked down in the faces all pink and eager and happy—I knew most of 'em by name. I'd be ashamed to live in a town where I didn't know anyway fifty-sixty children by name, keeping up as fast as necessary. And with 'em I see was Lisbeth's little boy, waving a stick of kindling for his wand, happy as a clam, but not a mum clam at all.

"Hello, Chris!" I says. "I didn't know you could drill."

But he stopped jumping and laughing. "I can't," he says, "I was just pe-tend. I can pe-tend, can't I?" he says, looking up alarmed.

"Hush, Calliope!" says Mis' Sykes, back of me. "No need making it any harder for him than 'tis."

"What do you mean by that?" I ask' her sharp.

"Why," says she, "I couldn't have him in the drill. How could I? The children's mothers is coming down here to trim 'em. Lots of 'em—Mis' Grace and Mis' Morgan Graves and some more, said flat out they wouldn't let their children be in it if they had to trim 'em along with her."

"My land," I says, "my land!"

I couldn't say anything more. And Mis' Sykes called the children, and they all went shouting round her over to the middle of the green. All but Chris.

I picked him up and set him on the counter of the booth, and I stood side of him. But he didn't pay much attention to me. He was looking off after the children, forming in two lines that broke into four, and wheeled and turned, and waved their wands. He watched 'em, and he never says a word.

"Come and help me tack tacks, Chris," I says, when I couldn't stand it any longer.

And then he says: "When they do it, it's going to be a band playing, won't there?"

"Yes," I says, "but we'll all be hearing the music. Come and——"

"When they do it," he says, still looking off at the children, "they'll all have white on 'em, won't they?"

"Yes," I says, "white on 'em." And couldn't say no more.

Then he turns and looks me right in the face: "I got my new white suit home," he says, whispering.

"Yes, lambin', yes," I says, and had to pretend I didn't understand. And when I looked back at him, he was setting there, still and watching; but two big tears was going down his cheeks.

All of a sudden something in me, something big and quiet, turned round to me and said something. I heard it—oh, I tell you, I heard it. And it wasn't the first time. And all over me went racing the knowledge that there was something to do for what was the matter. And while I stood there, feeling the glory of knowing that I'd got to find a way to do, somehow—like you do sometimes—to make things better, I looked down the long green stretch of the Square and in the middle of the Square I saw something. Something that was like an answer. And I put my arms round Chris and hugged him. For I'd got a plan that was like a present.

But he didn't feel like that—not then. He kind of wriggled away. "It ain't lovin' time," he says. "No."

"No," I says, looking down that sunny Market Square toward what I'd seen. "No, it ain't loving time—not yet. But I tell you, I tell you it's going to be it! Mebbe I can make 'em see—mebbe I know a way to make 'em see. Come along with me," I says, "Lisbeth's little boy—and help!"

Toward sundown of that first great day of the Friendship Village Home-coming we was the happiest, wore-outest set of folks I about ever see. Not everybody we'd expected and hoped for had come—even Abner Dawes, he hadn't showed up. But then he was such a big man that I donno's any of us thought he'd come, any of the time. Only we did enjoy having it in the *Daily* every few nights that he'd be there. The editor of the Friendship *Evening Daily* got six distinct locals out of it for "Supper Table Jottings"—six nights hand-running. Thus:

1. Abner Dawes is expected to arrive from the east for the Home-coming.

2. Abner Dawes will arrive from the east the last of the week. The occasion is the Home-coming.

3. Word has been received that Abner Dawes will reach here Thursday evening to attend the Home-coming.

4. Abner Dawes will reach here to-morrow night.

5. Abner Dawes will reach here this evening on the Six fifty-nine, for a brief sojourn.

6. Abner Dawes arrived last evening and is quartered at the Opera House hotel.

Some we hadn't thought of turned up last minute, and had to tell folks who they were and then—my, what a welcome! Every few minutes, all day long, we'd hear a little shouting, and see a little crowd, and we'd all rush over, and there'd be somebody just got there, and everybody'd be calling 'em old names, and shaking hands with the children and kissing the grandchildren. It was a real day. It'd be a day I'd like to talk about even if nothing else had happened but the day being just the day.

Mis' Sykes and I were in Eppleby's booth, and in back of it the children was all trimmed and ready to begin their march, when I heard an unusual disturbance just outside. I looked, and I saw Lisbeth, that Eppleby had asked to come and help tend his booth that night, and she was just getting there, with Chris trotting alongside of her. But they weren't making the disturbance. Most of that was Eppleby, shaking both the hands of a big, smooth-boned, brown-skinned man that was shouting at his lungs' top:

"Eppleby Bebbleby
Wooden-leg,
Lost his knife
Playing mumblety-peg."

with all the gusto of a psalm. And Eppleby was shouting back at him something about

"Abner Dawes he comes to late
The wood was split and things was great."

And it was Abner actually come and getting himself welcomed by Eppleby just like one of us. And Abner begun remembering us all and calling us by name.

Abner was one of them men that makes you know what men were meant to be like. His face was ruddy and wrinkled—but oh, it was deep and bright, and his eyes looked out like his soul was saying to your soul: "See me. I'm you. Oh, come on, let's find out about living. How does anybody ever talk about anything else?" That was Abner. You couldn't be with him without looking closer at the nature of being alive. And you saw that life is a different thing—a different thing from what most of us think. And some day we'll find out what.

And me, seeing him, and the folks all gathered round the Square, waiting for the after-supper part of the entertainment, and knowing what I'd planned should happen right afterward, I had only one thought:

"Abner," I says, just the same as if he hadn't been a great man, "the children—they're going to march. They're in back of the booth, all ready. You must lead 'em! He must lead 'em, Mis' Sykes, mustn't he—and sing with 'em? Every child here knows your songs. Oh, *would* you come and march with 'em?"

I love to remember how deep and bright his face got. "Would I march?" he says. "With *children*? When is it?—now?"

I put out my hand to thank him, and he took hold of it. And all of a sudden, right down there close by our two hands I see somebody. And it was Lisbeth's little boy, that had come running to us and was tugging at my skirt.

"Look," Chris says, clear. "I got on this white one. Couldn't— couldn't I march too?"

He was looking up, same as a rose, his big eyes shining hopeful. My, my, but he was dear. And Abner Dawes looked down at him. He'd never seen him before—nor knew about his being Lisbeth's.

"March!" Abner cries. "Of course you can march! Come along with me."

And he swung little Christopher up on to his back. And he run out into the midst of the other children, where Mis' Sykes was marshaling 'em before the booth.

"God bless him," says Eppleby, behind me.

But then Mis' Sykes looked up, and saw him. And she never hesitated a minute, not even a minute to wonder why. She just set her lips together in that thin line I knew, and she run right up to Abner.

"Oh, Mr. Dawes," she says, "you mustn't. The mothers won't like it. He's Lisbeth Note's child. He's———"

Abner Dawes looked down at her, round Chris's white legs. All the brightness was gone out of Abner's face now—but not the deepness nor the kindness. That stayed. "Do you mean," he said grave, "that this child is evil?"

"No—no," says Mis' Sykes, stumbling some. "But I thought you'd ought to know—folks feeling as they do here———"

Abner turned and looked down the green, where the folks was gathered and the last sun was slanting. It was gold, and it was still, all except the folks chatting in groups. And up the street the half-past seven bell was ringing, like somebody saying something nice.

"Oh, God," says Abner Dawes, kind of reverent and kind of like a sigh. "Here too. Here too."

I'll never forget his face when he turned to Mis' Sykes. It wasn't hard or cross or accusing—I guess he knew she was just at her crooked way of trying to be decent! But he made her know firm that if he led the children's march, he'd lead it with Chris.—And it was so he done.

...Down the long green they come, side by side. And the other children fell in behind, and they circled out into a great orbit, with the Christmas tree in the middle of it. And folks begun to see who the man was at the head, and the word run round, and they all broke out and cheered and called out to him. Oh, it was a great minute. I like to think about it.

And then the murmur begun running round that it was Chris that was with him. And Mame Holcomb and Eppleby and Mis' Toplady and me, watching from the booth, we knew how everybody was looking at everybody else to see what to think—like folks do. But they didn't know—not yet.

Then something wonderful happened. Halfway round the Square, Abner noticed that Chris didn't have any wand, same as the other children had. And so, when he was passing the big Cedar-of-Lebanon-looking Christmas tree, what did he do but break off a little branch and put that in Chris's hand. And Chris come on a-waving it, a bough off that tree. I sort of sung all over when I saw that.

The children ended up round a platform, and up there went the folks that had been picked out to lead the singing. And as they went they sung:

"Oh, how lovely is the evening, is the evening, is the evening!"

And in a minute, from first one place and then another the others took it up, them that had sung it in singing school, years ago—

"When the bells are sweetly chiming, sweetly chiming, sweetly chiming"

and they sung it like a round, which it is, with a great fine booming bass of

"Ding dong, ding dong, ding dong"

all through it. Do you know that round? If you don't, get it; and get some folks together somehow, and sing it. It lets you taste the evening. But I can't tell you the way it seemed to us there in Friendship Village, met together after so many years, and singing together like we was all one Folk. One Folk.

They sung other songs, while the dusk came on. Abner Dawes was sitting on the platform, and he kept Chris on his knee—I loved him for that. There wasn't a set program. First one would start a song from somewheres in the crowd, and then another.... And all the time I was waiting for it to get dark enough to do what I had planned to be done—and what I'd had men working at near all the night before to get ready. And when the dark come thick enough, and just at the end, I remember of their singing "Flow Gently, Sweet Afton," I thought it was time.

I gave the word to them that were waiting. And suddenly, right there in the midst of the Square, the great green tree, that had been the Friendship Village Christmas tree, glowed softly alight from top to bottom, all in the green branches, just like it had glowed on Christmas Eve. They'd done the work good, and as if they liked it—and the bulbs were in so deep in the green that not a soul had noticed all day. And there was the Christmas tree, come back.

"Oh...." they says, low, all over the Square. And nobody said anything else. It was as if, awake and alive in that living tree, there was the same spirit that had been there on Christmas Eve, the spirit that we've got to keep alive year long, year round, year through.

I'd whispered something to Abner, and he come down from the platform and went over close to the tree. And of a sudden he lifted Chris in his arms, high up among the lit branches. And in everybody's hush he says clear:

" *'And He took a little child and set him in their midst.'* "

That was all he said. And Chris looked out and smiled happy, and waved his branch off the Christmas tree. Over the whole Market Square there lay a stillness that said things to itself and to us. It said that here was the Family, come home, round the tree, big folks and little, wise and foolish, and all feeling the Christmas spirit in our hearts just like it *was* our hearts. It said that the Family's judging Lisbeth Note one way or the other didn't settle anything, nor neither did our treating her little boy mean or good....

For all of a sudden we were all of us miles deeper into life than that. And we saw how, beyond judgment and even beyond what's what, is a spirit that has got to come and clutch hold of life before such wrongs, and more wrongs, and all the wrongs that ail us, can stop being. And that spirit will be the spirit that was in our hearts right then. We all knew it together— I think even Mis' Sykes knew—and we stood there steeped in the knowing. And it was one of the minutes when the thing we've made out of living falls clean away, like a husk and a shell, and the Shining Thing inside comes close and says: "This is the way I am if you'll let me be it."

Away over on the edge of the Square somebody's voice, a man's voice—we never knew who it was—begun singing "Home Again, From a Distant Shore." And everybody all over took it up soft. And standing there round the Christmas tree in the middle of June, with that little child in our midst, it was as true for us as ever it was on Christmas night, that glory shone around. And we had come Home in more senses than we'd thought, to a place, a Great Place, that was waiting for us.

Pretty soon I slipped away, inside Eppleby's booth. And there, in all that scarlet bunting, Lisbeth stood, looking and crying, all alone—but crying for being glad.

"Lisbeth, Lisbeth!" I said, "right out there is the way life is—*when we can get it uncovered.*"

She looked up at me; and I saw the thing in her face that was in the faces of all those in the Square, like believing and like hoping, more than any of us knows how—yet.

"Honest?" she said. "Honest and truly?"

"Honest and truly," I told her.

And I believe that. And you believe it. If only we can get it said....

CPSIA information can be obtained
at www.ICGtesting.com
Printed in the USA
LVHW040557081222
734780LV00030B/1014